Political Origins of the U. S. Income Tax

Political Origins of
the U.S. Income Tax

by Jerold L. Waltman

UNIVERSITY PRESS OF MISSISSIPPI

JACKSON

Copyright © 1985 by the University Press of Mississippi
Manufactured in the United States of America

*This book has been sponsored by the
University of Southern Mississippi*

Library of Congress Cataloging in Publication Data

Waltman, Jerold L., 1945–
 Political origins of the U.S. income tax.
Includes index.
 1. Income tax—Law and legislation—United States—
History. 2. Income tax—United States—History.
I. Title. II. Title: Political origins of the US
income tax.
KF6369.W33   1985   343.7305'2'09   84-13100
ISBN 0-87805-245-3   347.3035209

To Timothy and Amy

Contents

Preface

The making of tax policy is much like a series of games. Every few years political and/or economic circumstances lead tax policy makers into a rewriting of the revenue code. As the resulting bill proceeds through the maze of legislative politics, the game becomes intense and complex. When the bill is finally sent to the president, the participants are usually exhausted and relieved that it is all over. However, no one is ever entirely satisfied, and preparations begin almost immediately for the next encounter which is sure to come in due course.

This book is about the first few such games of which the income tax was a part. Much of the story is of the growing importance and increasing rates of income taxation necessitated by the war. However, each revenue bill also carried important changes in the content of the income tax law. Several central issues, most notably the exclusion of municipal bond interest, were settled in such a way as to inhibit future reform. More issues were not, nor can they be, "settled," and are still very much with us. In addition, during these eight years there were changes in the way income tax policy was formulated. In short, substantive changes led to new political configurations, which in turn led to additional substantive changes. Specifically, the economic exigencies of the first World War led to a broadening of the coverage and a steep increase in the rates. These moves had the twin effect of bringing new interest groups into the political fray and raising the stakes of income tax politics. Naturally, this new political process had an impact on the substance of tax policy. The result was an income tax law far removed from the goals of its original authors.

If a political historian wishes to address an audience beyond those who share his narrow specialization, he may pursue one or both of two paths. One is drawing generalizations from his findings and tying these to theoretical material in political science; the other is making an attempt to relate the topic to matters of current interest. The first I have undertaken in the concluding chapter by developing a typology of tax politics, the second by sprinkling the narrative with notes on subsequent attempts to deal with the issue under consideration and a number of current dilemmas. I hope these will serve to elucidate, if nothing else, both the continuity and the intractability of problems in tax policy.

It is a pleasure to acknowledge some of the debts I have incurred producing this monograph. A summer grant from the University of Southern Mississippi gave me a block of time to do research. Librarians at Louisiana State University and the University of Southern Mississippi were most helpful. Among them, Paul McCarver of the governments documents section at Southern Mississippi should be singled out for a special thanks. His knowledge, good humor, and unfailing courtesy made the often tedious research much easier. Several people, particularly Ronald King and Edward Wheat, have read all or portions of the manuscript. They are owed thanks and an assurance that where I did not follow their advice the manuscript is probably that much weaker—as well as my responsibility.

Diane VanZandt provided a trio of services. For one, she turned my fragmented drafts into final typed copy. She also smoothed out the prose and saved me from several errors through her meticulous knowledge of the tax code.

Lastly, my family must be thanked for their usual forbearance and patience.

Political Origins of the U. S. Income Tax

I

Economics, Policy Making, and the 1913 Law

TAXATION is at the base of the nexus between governors and governed. Governments have always had to extract resources from their people, something which is seldom a pleasant task for either governments or taxpayers. People almost universally resent—an occasional Oliver Wendell Holmes aside—paying taxes, and governments, usually wary of potential uprisings, approach this task with some trepidation.

Popular government in America began over taxation, and to some extent taxation with representation has mitigated the worst features of oppressive taxation and violent resistance to it. Not that our political history has been free of passionate and sometimes violent (e.g., the Whiskey Rebellion) disputes over taxation. Quite the contrary. Taxation forever has been and always will be a subject of acute political controversy.

The income tax was first tried as an emergency revenue measure during the Civil War.[1] After that financial exigency, the political pressure to lower taxes resulted in its repeal in 1872. With the coming of rapid industrialization during the latter half of the nineteenth century came the creation of new social classes, new social movements, and new political ideas. All these brought in their train new revenue demands and political demands that the federal government look elsewhere than to the tariff for its funds. The birth of the Populist movement in the early nineties revived interest in the income tax, as the tax became a cornerstone of Populist litany.

In 1894, a Democratic and Populist-dominated Congress attached an income tax amendment to the tariff bill.[2] A vituperative attack began against the measure, an attack made more intense in that the tax was purposely designed to apply to only approximately 5 percent of the nation's taxpayers. Cries of "confiscation" were echoed throughout the land, to which Populist orators usually replied that these huge incomes were "stolen" anyway.

The following year, in one of its most celebrated cases, the Supreme Court struck down the law as unconsitutional.[3] The income tax, the court reasoned, levied a tax on rents, which were received because of landownership. The landowning origins of the base of the tax made it a tax on land. According to the Court's view of history, the Founding Fathers had equated a land tax with a direct tax. On this matter, the Constitution specified that any direct tax levied by the national government had to be apportioned among the states on the basis of population. Therefore, since the income tax was not so apportioned, it was unconstitutional.

The specious character of the Court's logic and its curious fund of historical knowledge have been thoroughly discussed and dissected.[4] Yet, given the political passions surrounding the issue and the backgrounds of the justices, the result is not entirely surprising. Faced with a self-styled attack on wealth and property, they reacted in like manner. Caught up in these turbulences, Justice Field wrote,

> The present assault upon capital is but the beginning. It will be but the stepping stone to others, larger and more sweeping, till our political contests will become a war of the poor against the rich.[5]

Although the proposal's backers refused to believe the Court had spoken the last word and wanted to repass the law, they were unable to secure the necessary backing in Congress. With McKinley's election, a veto would have been likely in any event. Over the years, the measure slipped onto the political system's back burner, although a few die-hard adherents futilely offered income tax bills every time Congress met.

The Progressive movement came to endorse the idea, though,

and served to keep it alive. Foreign countries continued their income taxes, feeling few of the ill-effects the wealthy had claimed would certainly befall the nation with its adoption. Professional economists continued to talk about the tax and to support its adoption. In short, the idea would not die.

In 1909, an unusual situation developed which opened the door to national taxation of American incomes. President Taft sincerely believed that the Republican Party, under the banner of protectionism, had pushed tariffs too high for its own good.[6] At the same time, an intraparty dispute had been going on in Congress for several years between progressive, mostly midwestern and western, and Old Guard, mostly east coast, Republicans. On the Democratic side, that party's absorption of the Populist remnant after the 1896 election had seated a number of men of rather radical temperament among them.

When Congress convened that year, Taft had high hopes for tariff reform. The Republican-dominated House Ways and Means Committee produced a bill which contained only a few reductions, but which Taft and most moderate Republicans thought they could live with. Ignoring this measure entirely, Nelson W. Aldrich, the powerful chairman of the Senate Finance Committee, drew up his own bill which actually raised tariffs. The progressive wing of the party was outraged and a frontal assault on Aldrich and his bill erupted in the Senate.[7] Some Democratic leaders suggested quietly that the ultimate embarrassment would be to attach an income tax amendment to this bill and the "insurgents" agreed. Backed by this coalition, the income tax now stood a fair chance of being enacted.

Realizing that he had uncorked a genie, Aldrich met hurriedly with Taft, who he knew feared for the Supreme Court's reputation if it had to rule again on the income tax. The two concocted an unusual strategy to defeat the measure: They would sponsor a constitutional amendment to allow Congress to levy an income tax, hoping such a move would take some of the steam out of the Democratic-Insurgent strength. The ploy worked. The amendment glided through Congress, sponsored by the income tax's opponents, and the income tax bill, backed by its friends, died.[8]

In common with many other best-laid plans, this one went awry.

One state after another ratified the amendment, and four years later it had received the number of assents necessary to become the Sixteenth Amendment to the Constitution.[9] By this time, Woodrow Wilson was in the White House and the Democrats in control of Congress. While opponents in and out of Congress still flailed away at the income tax, it was easily attached to the new tariff bill.

Born of a partisan movement to achieve social justice, its revenue potential was not considered of paramount value. With the onset of World War I, however, the income tax proved its mettle as a revenue raiser. That conflict worked a revolution in American fiscal affairs, with the income tax emerging from it as the mainstay of the revenue system. From that point on there has been no serious movement to repeal it.

But policies and laws do not remain static. Just as changed social and economic conditions created a demand for an income tax in the first place, so too would a host of factors create demands to alter its various provisions.

To be able to appreciate these changes, a backdrop of three things must be provided: 1)a survey of the economics and legalities of income taxation, 2)a review of the structure of tax policy making in the 1913–21 era, and 3)an overview of the provisions of the 1913 law.

Economics and Legalities

Utilizing income as a tax base means first that the term must be defined. Economic theorists have approached this problem from several angles.[10] Some have argued that the key problem is constructing a definition that will differentiate income from capital (individual and aggregate). Others have taken the view that psychic satisfactions are the real elements of income; that is, people only seek economic goods for the psychic rewards they derive from them, not as ends in themselves. According to still others, income is what is spent on consumption. Another set of theorists has sought to divine the increase in social goods (or total productivity if you will) during a period, then define income as each person's share of that aggregate increase.

By far the most widely accepted concept, however, in the United States is that developed by Robert Haig and Henry Simons. Dispensing with problems of aggregate measurement and notions of capital maintenance, they defined income as the increase in economic power a person enjoyed over a given time period. Simons said the following:

> Personal income may be defined as the algebraic sum of 1)the market value of rights exercised in consumption and 2)the change in value of the store of property rights between the beginning and end of the period in question. In other words, it is merely the result obtained by adding consumption during the period to "wealth" at the end of the period and then subtracting "wealth" at the beginning.[11]

Similarly, Haig defined income as

> the increase or accretion to one's power to satisfy his wants in a given period in so far as that power consist of a)money itself or b)anything susceptible of valuation in terms of money. More simply stated, the definition of income which the economist offers is this: Income is the *money value of the net accretion to one's economic power between two points of time.*[12]

To adopt this as a beginning point for the levying of a tax settles several economic problems but not all. Moreover, designing a statute and an administrative system to implement it present numerous difficulties. First, what about self-generated goods and services? The farmer who grows his own food has earned income according to the definition. But has the gardener who grows flowers? "Economic power" for Haig or "wealth" for Simons may be the decisive factor here, but both these terms ultimately connote satisfactions. That is, someone somewhere might pay a handsome sum for the flowers. Who is to say, then, whether things done for pleasure constitute more "wealth" than things done for more utilitarian purposes. Could it be that a line should be drawn between the potatoes the farmer grows and the artichokes? What, to draw another example, of the person who paints his own house? Income to be sure, but how to levy a tax on activities of this sort?

To omit all self-generated income in kind, a logical compromise with practicality, creates its own anomalies. What about exchanges in kind? Is the situation fundamentally different if a farmer shares some food with his neighbor and the neighbor helps him paint his house? The answer is of course not; but to allow this type of activity to escape taxation gives a powerful incentive to avoid the tax by barter.

Another problem is created by fluctuations in the value of property. If a person has 100 shares of stock which are worth $100 per share on January 1 and $150 per share on December 31, he clearly has an income of $5000. His "economic power" or "wealth" has increased by that much. However, to try to write a tax law which required every taxpayer to revalue everything he owned every year would create enormous difficulties. Inflation or deflation of the currency during a year, or part of it, presents similar problems. Assume on March 1 a dollar is worth 20 percent more than it was on January 1 but by December 31 is back to its original value. No income? What of the man who sold dollars on a foreign currency exchange on March 1 and bought them back December 31? If this is not income, are any gains from speculations income?

Other issues arise by the emphasis the definition puts on money and exchanges as measuring devices. The classic example is a bachelor who pays a housekeeper. Two incomes are created. If he marries the housekeeper, the economic position is the same, but income has fallen. Further, some types of receipts are difficult to label as income. Life insurance proceeds are one example. And what of gratuities, especially those which merely spread purchasing power among closely related persons. Is a father's gift to a child income to the child?

Capital gains present an especially vexing problem.[13] If income is defined as gains accruing during a given period (usually a year) and if there is a distinction between capital and income, consider the following case: A person buys a piece of real estate. After five years it doubles in value. He waits another five years to sell it, during which time its value remains stable. Has he received any income? Definitions of income which insist on a differentiation between capital and income and most income tax laws would answer in the negative, classifying this as capital accretion and not income. The Haig-Simons definition, however, would include these gains. Theoretically, the amount of each year's appreciation in value should be included in that year's income, but a reasonable administrative compromise with pristine theory is to recognize it for tax purposes in the year in which a sale is made. If the property is not sold but is passed to an heir, assuming that inheritances are to be included in income, what is the amount of the income to the heir?

A further legal wrinkle, troublesome particularly in the early years of the American tax, was introduced because of some British statutory provisions and court decisions. The British defined income in such a way that capital gains were excluded; hence there was some worry that the tax allowed by the Sixteenth Amendment would not allow capital gains taxation unless the statute were carefully drawn in its definition of income. Furthermore, in both Britain and America land taxes had always had a somewhat different legal status than levies on other types of properties. Capital gains taxation of land transactions might therefore be subject to even more careful scrutiny by the courts. In time, both these issues were settled by the courts deferring to Congress's definition of income. However, in the early years of the law's life, this outcome was by no means certain.

If we are now agreed that all gains should be included in income (even if recognition is postponed), what about losses? The case of the businessman seeking to figure his "net profit" is fairly clear. If he is a specialty manufacturer who makes twenty dumafligits during a year, making a profit on eighteen but suffering a loss on two, he may fairly deduct the loss from his profits on the others. But what if the businessman is also a speculator in grain futures? His gains are taxable. But what if he has a net loss for the year? Another person, a worker at the factory, sells his dining room table for more than he paid for it. A taxable gain is created. He sells a bookshelf for less than he paid for it. A deductible loss?

If we try to draw a line between business transactions and personal ones, the problem of assets that are transferred crops up. A person starts a business and uses his previously personal truck solely for business purposes. Suppose he sells it two years later. What is its basis? The original cost? The fair market value when it became a business asset? The basis it would have had had depreciation been deducted during the years of personal use?

After a legally satisfactory definition of income has given us the base of the tax, the next step is to construct the rates. The three possibilities are regressive rates, proportional rates, and progressive rates. However, hardly anyone advocates regressive taxation in principle (although many tax systems have been and are in practice).

The political philosophy underlying income taxation has been in fact linked closely to progressive taxation.[14] For both proponents and opponents this was its major attraction or repulsion. While in recent years the idea of a proportional income tax has had some backers,[15] during the period covered by the present effort, progression was an accepted feature, the question being only how much.

While this is not the place to go into detail concerning the arguments for and against progressive taxation, they need to be mentioned because they shaped the continuing political battle over what the rates should be.

One of the key supporting arguments for progression in income taxes, especially in the early years, was that it helped to offset the regressive character of other taxes, especially the customs duties. Customs duties had the double effect of taxing consumers through higher prices and enriching American manufacturers. A graduated income tax, therefore, would redress this inequity.

On a more general plane, it has long been argued that the doctrine of "equal sacrifice" should be applied in taxation. Taking 10 percent of a poor person's income requires more of a sacrifice from him than is required of a wealthy person from whom 10 percent of income is taken. Therefore, to equalize the burden, a higher percentage of income must be taken as the amount of income climbs. Another column upon which progressive taxation can be made to rest is the idea that the wealthy receive more benefits from government expenditure than do people with lower incomes. Thus, maintaining order, providing fire protection, and so forth are more beneficial to large property owners since they have more to protect.[16]

Two arguments loaded with politically explosive material have also been advocated. One is that the social value of the expenditures of people with low incomes is greater than that of the more fortunately situated. The poor spend their meager incomes on food, clothing, and shelter, while the rich spend much on frivolous luxuries. Hence, taking away part of this spending power of the rich cuts down on the waste of societal resources. The other, simply stated, is that a progressive tax lessens economic inequality, which is seen by definition as an unnecessary evil.

The objections to progressive taxation are usually concentrated in three areas. First, progressive taxation undeniably complicates the tax law and its administration. A progressive tax schedule will provide economic incentives for ingenuity in devising ways to get around its effects. The more graduated the scale, of course, the greater the premium put on such ingenuity. Then, trying to construct laws and administrative regulations to counteract these moves, requiring equal ingenuity, will consume inordinate amounts of time. Two brief examples will perhaps make this problem clearer.

If A is in a 50 percent marginal bracket and B in a 25 percent bracket, for each dollar of income A can have attributed to B, he saves 25¢. Now, if B is A's wife, child, or other relative, he really may not suffer any diminution of purchasing power. The ways he can accomplish this are limited only by competent legal counsel's imagination, especially if a good part of his income consists of dividends, interest, and capital gains. Another area is the timing of income. If a person's income is high this year, he may try to have some of it shifted to next year when he anticipates a lower income. Again, any number of schemes are readily at hand to manage this. A great deal of society's talents go, therefore, into the totally nonproductive task of tax avoidance.

A second objection is that it leads to political irresponsibility. One view is that the majority can levy higher and higher taxes on a minority (the wealthy), ultimately taking, under the guise of taxation, all income above a certain level. Another is that if the majority do not pay the taxes but do vote how the money is spent, one of the key supports of popular government is removed. Detaching the paying of taxes from the power to spend money is to invite irresponsibility in its spending.

A third objection is that progressive taxation damages economic incentives. As marginal tax rates climb, a person has less and less incentive to work. Since he can keep fewer and fewer of the dollars he earns, at some point he will prefer leisure to working. This point, the argument goes, is reached much sooner under progressive than proportional taxation. High graduated rates also have a deleterious effect on capital accumulation, it is contended. Economic productivity, which as the argument goes is beneficial to all, is enhanced by capital investment, which comes from savings. Since persons with high incomes have a higher propensity to save than persons with lower incomes, graduated taxes eat away at a portion of would-be capital.

All of the arguments, pro and con, have been stated here in very simple form and without rebuttal. All of them admit of more complexity and of qualifications and counter-arguments. However, they invariably arise when the question comes up, as it always does, what shall the rate structure be?

Part of the question of rates is the matter of the exemption. A strong case can be made that persons on subsistence incomes should be granted an exemption. However, exactly where the exemption should be set runs amuck of other questions. By what standards do we measure subsistence (or poverty level)? Should a tax be as nearly universal as possible? Should all persons, even the poorest, contribute something in support of government to establish a claim that their voice should be heard in decision making? Should the incidence of other taxes be taken into account when setting the exemption?

Turning from questions of base and rate, there are three other questions which bedevil economic analysis. First, should all income be taxed at the same rate? Take the difference between earned and unearned income. One argument has it that earned income should be taxed more lightly since it derives from more socially useful activity. Others, with equal fervor, say this creates a tax penalty against those who must invest to keep the engines of production going. Capital gains, as another example, should be singled out for special treatment according to some. To do so gives an incentive for people to buy capital assets. Further, not to do so means, since many holders of capital assets are in high marginal brackets, that people will worry too much about the tax impacts of their sales and the economy will not function normally. Others see little merit in these positions, contending capital gains produce income just like any other gain.

Second, should all persons who receive the same income be taxed alike? Should a married person have an additional exemption, or part of one, for a nonworking spouse? Should family size matter? A third question is whether how one's income is spent should affect his taxes. Usually, the argument is that for some sorts of expenditures a deduction or credit ought to be allowed. For example, what about gifts to charitable institutions? These institutions undoubtedly contribute to the public good. But does that make a backhanded subsidy by government justifiable? (Deductions reduce one person's taxes, thereby necessitating that others pay more if equivalent revenues are to be maintained.) Or, what about unusual expenditures that befall a particular taxpayer, such as heavy medical expenses? A taxpayer's ability to pay is surely diminished by such an occurrence as a debilitating illness. But where to draw the line in such matters?

The third question spills over into the whole murky matter of using the tax system to encourage or discourage other activities. Most economists argue that the tax system ought to be restricted to the function of raising revenue. A plethora of other segments of society, however, see the tax system as an ideal way to encourage or discourage people to do or not to do whatever it is they want done or not done. The irony is that there is no way to do exactly what the economist wants because the tax system will inevitably affect how people arrange their affairs.

However, opening the tax system up to other policy objectives both has an impact on the revenue picture and complicates the tax policy making process. Revenue is obviously lowered by the granting of special credits, and the same observation made above about raising other people's taxes applies here. When a special tax is levied to discourage something, it seldom produces much revenue since the purpose in levying it was that people would not pay it. As for policy making, frequently a counter group will become active in opposing the credit or special tax—although this is much more likely in the latter than the former case since the impacts of the former are so slight and spread so widely. Even if such a group does not arise, the inevitable result is that a host of other groups will be encouraged to push for similar tax juggling concerning their favorite project. As will be seen momentarily, tax policy makers have enough forces to contend with, and adding these others may lead to system overload. Of course, whether better or worse tax policy is produced by this more complicated process is a matter of one's own judgment.

After all these economic matters are thrashed out, there remain a number of legal and administrative complications, some endemic to American conditions, others universal. There is, for one, the linkage between the corporation and personal income taxes. In 1913 Congress changed the Corporation Excise Tax to an income tax. This makes corporations pay the income tax in their capacity as legal persons. The earnings of corporations are then distributed to the stockholders as dividends. Even if we settle the thorny issue of whether or not this is double taxation, the legal and administrative difficulties are not few.

Another problem is the linkages between years. If the rates change, what about income earned in one year but recognized in another? Even with unvarying rates, some people will have fluctuating incomes and may end up paying more over a five-year period, for instance, than others with regular incomes but the same total amount. Then, there is the question of loss carryovers. Should a business loss in one year be deductible against next year's gain or is each year a discrete entity?

One of the most perplexing difficulties of income taxation is constructing ways to accurately measure business income. Given the diversity of the American economy, there are all sorts of businesses which operate in unusual ways. Trying to write general rules which will allow their incomes to be treated fairly in comparison with others is an almost impossible task. Accounting theory is usable to an extent. However, like any dynamic discipline this field is always in a state of flux. What were considered expenses before may now be seen as capital expenditures. A method of valuing inventory or calculating depreciation may be in and then out of favor. The special guidelines the accounting profession publishes for special types of businesses are especially open to changes. Hence, the tax code is always subject to the charge that its general principles create a hardship on this or that line of business, frequently with some justification. Of course, at the same time, any willingness on the part of tax writing officials to make exceptions for one type of business will bring dozens of others forward with proposals for their businesses. Naturally, many of these pleas have nothing to do with equity and are merely disguised attempts to escape taxation. However, sorting through them, with attendant political pressures, complicates the tax policy making process considerably.

Lastly, some mention must be made of the ramifications of our federal structure. *McCulloch v. Maryland* (1819) has always hung over those formulating tax policy in America. Being more than eager to avoid any adverse court decisions, the early drafters of the income tax read the decision in its most extreme form. For many years the salaries of state and local officials were not subjected to the tax. For more years the interest on state and local bonds has been exempt. Neither of these can be defended on economic grounds, and probably not on constitutional grounds, but they stood nevertheless.

In another vein, there has been some concern with how the federal income tax itself affects state and local income taxes. Since it has been shown to be by far the best revenue producer under modern economic conditions, will too heavy a reliance by federal authorities on an income tax deprive the states of an important revenue source? As early as the debate on the passage of the first income tax law, the idea of having the federal government collect income taxes but remit part of the proceeds to the states was raised.[17] Federal issues such as these, while sometimes muted, are never absent when the financing of government is discussed.[18]

Tax Policy Making, 1913–21

Shifting to the perspective of emprical political analysis presents a new set of questions. Who are the decision makers? What influences are they subject to? What is the structure of decision making?

Outside Influences

Following the organizing device of systems analysis, we are first led to ask what forces can bring about a demand for a change in the tax law.[19] One ever present factor is the government's revenue needs. If expenditures are slated to rise, these decision makers will be called upon to find the wherewithal. On the contrary, a budget surplus will generate calls to decrease taxes, and they must decide where to make the cuts. Another factor which casts an eternal spell over tax decision makers is the general state of the economy. A boom accompanied by inflation or a depression accompanied by deflation will almost always result in demands for alteration in fiscal policy. In this situation, tax policy will naturally become entwined with other economic policies.

More tangible but carrying equal import with politicians are elite and mass attitudes. Articulate elites talk, think, and write continually about public affairs.[20] At any given point in time, elites will hold what might be labeled a "public philosophy" which conditions political debate and sets the contours of the acceptable alternatives. In this period in particular "Progressivism" is the best epithet to describe the prevalent public philosophy, for even those who fought it did so in terms that the Progressives defined.

While government is heavily influenced by elites, most politicians have at least one eye on the masses. It may be true that the masses do not have much direct impact on public policy; but it is equally true that politicians weigh electoral factors into their decisions. Hence, their reading of the "public mood," while it was even more vague in those days than now, is certainly a factor when decisions regarding public policy are made. And, of course, the ephemeral character of this public mood, as well as politicians' perceptions of it, is legendary. Thus, perceived changes in its nature and direction can have a decided impact on changes in tax policy.

From its inception, our income tax policy has been continually analyzed by economists. Since its development began about the same time economics was becoming established as a distinct discipline, perhaps the marriage was inevitable. Whatever the reason, economists have had no hesitancy about recommending changes in the law to bring various parts of it more into accord with their own economic theory. Their writings consequently have more often than not been addressed to both other economists and policy makers; and a reading of the floor debates will show that the latter do indeed digest these pieces. Further, economists were often called upon by congressmen for advice in the early days and, as the Treasury augmented its staff, by the executive branch. Almost every economist prominent during this period in public finance worked for a time for either the Treasury or a congressional committee.[21]

Interest groups are always active in tax policy, as would be expected. As soon as the income tax was adopted, virtually every business trade association set up a tax committee or hired a full time person to keep abreast of tax changes. It was but a short step to making suggestions to Congress and engaging in lobbying. General interest business groups, such as the Chamber of Commerce, did likewise. Furthermore, many large business firms had someone on their staff, or retained an attorney, to be their spokesman on tax matters.

Then there have always been public interest groups with an interest in taxation. Usually, though, they have been small and ill-financed. Consequently, their role has normally been marginal. More important have been accountants and lawyers and their professional groups. During this period, they, especially the accountants, confined their activities to matters purely technical in nature. However, their concerns usually dealt only with tax questions affecting those with large incomes. In addition, there have always been plenty of special interest groups who have wanted to use the tax system to achieve some other policy goal.

Decisions of the courts can generate demands for change, especially if they hold a section of a statute unconstitutional or if they interpret the statute in ways unintended by Congress. Sometimes, though, the courts will merely be applying the tax law to some novel situation, and whatever they decide will stimulate calls for Congress to clarify the matter. Similarly, administrative rulings can do likewise. It was (and is) the normal course of events that when the commissioner made a ruling that adversely affects numerous taxpayers they came to Congress to press their case.

The Structure of Decision Making

The first factor to be entered into the equation is the constitutional position of the House. Article 1, Section 7 provides: "All Bills for raising Revenue shall originate in the House of Representatives; but the Senate may propose or concur with Amendments as on other Bills."

With the legacy of the revolution and Shay's Rebellion in memory, placing the power to tax in the hands of the most representative branch of government was an important move. In the scheme of government the Founding Fathers erected around it, this had a twin effect. First, it made the House the most important arena for the initiation of tax policy. Second, because that was the only special power accorded the House, it meant that it would be guarded with a special jealousy. The prestige of the House vis-à-vis the Senate and the executive branch is frequently on the line in matters of tax policy.

As befits this premier role, the House Ways and Means Committee has always been a centerpiece of the House committee structure. A seat on this prestigious group has been a prize since the early days of the Republic. Relative to the House as a whole, it is always one of the most powerful, and usually the most powerful, of House committees.[22] Certainly 1913–1921 was not a period of diminished power for this committee; if anything, it was one of its brighter eras.

The ratio of party assignments to Ways and Means and the choice of a chairman followed the same percentage arrangements as those of other committees, meaning the majority party controlled both. Within the parties, the members of Ways and Means occupied important positions. Thus, party politics and tax politics became inextricably intertwined. When there was a consensus among the Ways and Means people, they could easily control the caucus. Conversely, when a dispute erupted among the majority on Ways and Means, it was almost sure to become a bitter intraparty fight.

Political parties occupied a pivotal role in the 1913–21 Congresses. Party discipline, even though it had begun its decline, was very important. Each party held regular caucuses in each house, making decisions which were often, technically at least, binding on members' floor votes. In the House, for most of this period, the chairman of Ways and Means also chaired the caucus, making his power immense—as long as he held onto political influence. If his leadership of the party was challenged, it meant that tax policy would be the first area to feel the impact. Much depended then on the personality and political adroitness of the occupant of that seat.

Outside the House, the chairman was connected to several chains leading to other seats of power, the president, the secretary of the treasury, and the chairman of the Senate Finance Committee. The degree of influence he could exercise in these relationships depended on many factors, not the least of which was his political strength in the House.

For the president, the Ways and Means chairman can be a legislative leader for the administration and key party spokesman. On the other hand, he and the president may have differences, which was the case, for instance, during the war years. Turning to the secretary of the treasury, several factors are involved. If the president and the chairman are cool, the secretary cannot be too close to the chairman. If, though, the chairman's relationship with the White House is good, the two can be cooperative. On the other hand, there have been secretaries of the treasury who have been kept at a distance from the president, and this may make the Ways and Means head prefer to deal with the chief himself. Regarding the upper house, the Senate Finance chairman conferred frequently with him; however, Ways and Means chairmen have always endeavored to keep their Senate counterpart at arm's length, keeping the power of initiation firmly in their own hands. Although only two men, Claude Kitchin and Joseph Fordney, occupied this post from 1913 to 1921, as we shall see all these variables changed.

Ways and Means contained several subcommittees, the most important for our purposes being the one on Internal Taxation. As these years opened, income taxation was considered almost exclusively in this subcommittee, making its chairman rival his boss in influence. As the tax's role in the total revenue picture grew, however, the parent committee spent more and more time on it.

The Senate Finance Committee has always occupied a rather different position from Ways and Means. First, it has never been as powerful relative to the Senate as is Ways and Means relative to the House for the simple reason that revenue is not the Senate's primary bailiwick. While this is not to say that it was weak or unimportant, it is to say that its place was not at the center of the political stage. Moreover, the chairman did not command the position either on the committee or in the party that his House counterpart did. Senators consider themselves to be powerful as individuals, reducing the constraints on dissenting from the chairman's views. Furthermore, appeals from the committee to the caucus were not uncommon, something that in the House would have been pointless considering the dual role of the Ways and Means chairman. In the Senate, the Finance Committee chair was only one of several important personages with a say in caucus decisions.

The small size of the Finance Committee and this individualistic approach to the exercise of power made subcommittees somewhat less important. However, the Finance Committee's Subcommittee on Estate and Income Taxation and its chairman did exercise some influence. He was the one normally charged with the floor management of income tax bills; hence, he had to develop at least a modicum of expertise and a large repertoire of floor leadership skills.

Both the subcommittee and its parent were given over to extended discussion throughout this period. In part, this was necessary for the hallowed reason that every senator needed an opportunity to have his say; in part, it was necessary to develop some sort of consensus among strong-minded individuals. In addition, though, there was an ethos on the Finance Committee that the House versions of bills were hurriedly drawn and full of technical defects. Normally, therefore, a bill coming out of Finance was loaded down with amendments.

Consideration of revenue bills on the House floor did not produce much of significance. The Ways and Means chairman touched all bases well beforehand. A favorable rule had been secured from the Rules Committee. Noses were counted in the majority party and perhaps even a few of the minority coaxed into going along. Some floor time was allotted to the ranking minority member of Ways and Means to allow him and a few of his lieutenants to flail away at the evils of the bill. A few noncommittee amendments were always offered, but they were easily defeated. At the end, a favorable vote was but a final routine.

The Senate floor, on the other hand, was a more important arena. Just as the Finance Committee members did not hesitate to challenge their chairman, so too other senators did not hesitate to challenge the committee. The debate was a long and drawn out process, spiced by the offering of a barrage of amendments. The Finance chairman and Estate and Income chairman usually tried to fend off as many amendments as they could, though their success rate varied substantially. Party leaders often tried, as in the House, to freeze decisions taken there into binding floor votes. Following the Insurgent uprising of 1909, however, Senate party lines were broken more and more often. On more than one occasion, a dissident faction in the majority party would unite with the minority to overturn a Finance-approved provision.

At the critical stage of conference committee, the four chairmen of the revenue committees and subcommittees were always appointed, along with some of their other members. The Ways and Means chairman was typically in a strong position inasmuch as he was virtually the dictator of the House delegation. Also, it was usually his version of the bill the House had passed. Power was much more evenly distributed among the senators. Moreover, they sometimes had to bring in a bill containing provisions they did not want. Also, they had to be more careful because rejection of a conference committee report was always more likely in the Senate.

Turning to the executive branch, the first variable, as always, was the president himself. Seldom are presidents anything but novices in the intricacies of tax policy, and Wilson and Harding were no exceptions. Nevertheless, they had political leanings and some vague, general ideas on taxation. Too, since tax reform is an ever-popular issue, neither of these men when candidates missed the usual opportunity to say something about it during their campaigns. What happened was that the statement itself created political demands to promote tax reform once in office.

The unorganized character of the government's budget system of that day served to minimize presidential influence. President Taft's Commission on Economy and Efficiency had recommended the executive budget procedure that was to result in the Budget and Accounting Act of 1921, but in this period between the recommendation and its implementation the system was as inchoate as ever. Because they could not merge expenditure totals into a coherent program to present to Congress and match them with revenue estimates, both Wilson and Harding had to defer to Treasury estimates on the expenditure side and then confer with the secretary of the treasury and the Ways and Means chairman about how the revenue problems might be tackled. This disconnecting of the budget's two sides in the early stages of policy development deprived the president of a key weapon, the political initiative.

The secretary of the treasury has historically been second only to the secretary of state in prestige within the cabinet. From George Washington forward, occupants of the chief executive's post have in most cases leaned heavily on them in matters of financial policy. However, several factors determine the secrtary's standing in tax policy in general and income taxation in particular.

First, he may have little interest in tax matters and choose to work in other areas. Or, even if he has an interest in tax policy, economic conditions may dictate that he concentrate on other areas. Both of these situations occurred in this period. Of equal importance is his political standing, something else which varied during our period. At times, he was a close presidential adviser on economic matters; at others, the president simply deferred to him. In either case, his influence on tax policy was substantial. Alternatively, a president has sometimes chosen to use the secretary as a general political troubleshooter, which served to lessen the time he could devote to taxes. Naturally, too, it is normal for a secretary to have conflicts, personal and political, with other cabinet members, and these will occupy his time as well as affect his political standing.

Outside the executive branch, his relations with Congress and interest groups are of paramount importance and depend on a number of variables. In these years, the most important were his dealings with the chairman of Ways and Means. When they were of the same political party and political allies, their initial consultations determined the whole shape of the legislative package. On the contrary, if they were at odds, either the president had to step in or some compromise effected. Whatever the case, the outcome was affected by and affected the two men's political standing in their respective spheres. In terms of the Senate Finance Committee chairman, the variables were similar except that the interaction tended to occur after the initial bill had been drawn up.

Some secretaries come to office with important ties to interest groups, especially here Andrew Mellon. These were both valuable political assets and heavy liabilities. Within the administration, they served to strengthen the secretary's hand. The fact that these were powerful economic interest groups with actual or potential campaign contributions in hand was lost on few people.

On the other hand, when a powerful faction in Congress was opposed to these interest groups and the tax policies they stood for, the secretary's job of getting a bill through was made more difficult. The opposition sometimes came from the chairman of Ways and Means, sometimes from a group of powerful senators. Either way, the secretary had to tread gingerly and make critical compromises.

During the eight years under consideration here, there was no institutionalization of noncabinet advisers. Nonetheless, presidents have always had confidants who gave general personal and political advice, and these presidents followed this tradition. The importance of economic policy to political considerations meant that the role of these people sometimes rivaled the secretary of the treasury. Furthermore, tax and budget policy affect a number of other federal bureaucracies—Commerce, Interior, Labor, Agriculture, and State, to name the most important. On top of the usual bureaucratic infighting that is Washington's daily life, these agencies (or parts of them) may be tied to an interest group with a political ax to grind. Thus, it is not surprising that they tried to influence presidential positions and, failing that, did the usual leapfrog to their allies in Congress.

Within the Treasury itself, the secretary is not the only person of stature. He always had advisers and aides of various sorts to whom he was forced to turn for help in both technical and policy areas. In addition, there was the special position of the commissioner of Internal Revenue. As the implementation of the income tax proceeded, all sorts of administrative complexities developed, and the secretary had to look to the commissioner for suggested solutions. Too, congressional committees often called upon Treasury officials to testify, asking them their opinions and demanding that they defend proposals emanating from the Treasury. What all this added up to is that the Treasury was not a one man show and that policy positions taken by the secretary or the department may have represented internal compromise rather than the logical development of someone's thoughts.

In sum, the political process is multifaceted. The peculiar structure of American electoral politics can produce all sorts of combinations of people occupying the key roles. The internal politics of the administration and Congress can make one person more or less powerful at any given moment in time. Outside influences, from revenue needs to an article by a well-known economist, triggered demands for change. Added to these factors were administrative rulings, court decisions, and a dynamic economy producing all types of new business ventures daily. Change in tax codes is therefore endemic to taxation itself, but these demands must pass through the uncertain prism that is the tax policy making political subsystem.

The 1913 Law

To begin, the definition of income was as follows:

(G) ains, profits, and income derived from salaries, wages, or compensation for personal service of whatever kind and in whatever form paid, or from professions, vocations, businesses, trade, commerce, or sales, or dealings in property, whether real or personal, growing out of the ownership or use of or interest in real or personal property, also from interest, rent, dividends, securities, or the transaction of any lawful business, carried on for gain or profit, or gains or profits and income derived from any source whatever, including the income from but not the value of property acquired by gift, bequest, devise, or descent.

The broad character of the definition almost makes income synonomous with receipts. Self-generated income in kind was omitted, but not income in kind that was part of a transaction ("in whatever form paid").

Considerable ambiguity is evident on capital gains. A casual reading seems to indicate that they are taxable. However, Cordell Hull, the drafter of the statute, said that only the portion of the appreciation attributable to the year of sale was taxable.[23] And, the foremost authority on income taxes, writing soon after the act's passage, concurred with this assessment.[24] However, the Bureau of Internal Revenue began collecting the tax on all capital gains, and the Supreme Court agreed with this interpretation in a pair of key decisions in 1920 and 1921.[25] So whether or not intended, capital gains have been fully taxed from the beginning.

The receipt of money is not always income as defined here, though. Gifts and inheritances are excluded, as are proceeds from life insurance.[26]

One part of the definition which needs to be stressed is that *all* gains were taxed ("derived from any source whatever"), but that no provision was made for deduction of losses. Another question involves gambling winnings, since whether they are "gains, profits, or income" is debatable. (The commissioner ruled them taxable, however.) Also to be noted is that gains from illegal transactions were not taxable.

Lastly, all income is here treated alike. No differentiation is allowed for earned versus unearned or capital gains or any other type of receipt.

Certain persons and types of income were made exempt. The current president and all sitting federal judges were excluded because of the constitutional provision barring a decrease in their salaries.[27] Employees of state and local governments, as mentioned before, were exempted for fear of a court challenge. For the same reason, as well as the fact that it had been an objection raised in several state legislatures in the ratification of the Sixteenth Amendment, interest on state and local bonds was not to be included in income.

The law allowed several deductions to be taken. First, all "necessary" business expenses (paid but not accrued) could be taken off.

Second, all interest and taxes were deductible by both businesses and individuals. The reasoning behind this is not clear. One represents discretionary spending, while the other has nothing to do with income *per se*. Both, of course, have a bearing on disposable personal income, but then so do a variety of other factors not mentioned. One argument could be that these were legitimate business deductions, and individuals should have the same privilege. If that were the rationale, though, it could be extended to any number of other business expenses. A hole was created in the income tax base by these provisions, and it was a hole that was to be enlarged as the years went by.

Business, but not personal, losses were deductible, including those "arising from fire, storms, or shipwreck, and not compensated for by insurance or otherwise." A deduction was allowed for bad debts which the taxpayer wrote off as uncollectible. Incidentally, these were deductible whether or not the original cause for the debt produced any income.

The word "depreciation" was not mentioned, but a "reasonable allowance for the exhaustion, wear and tear of property arising out of its use or employment in the business" was allowed. However, the deduction could not be taken for expenses incurred in restoring the value of property if such a deduction were taken. This provision contains an important problem which will need to detain us briefly.

To the accountant the term "depreciation" means the *allocation of cost*. Assume a machine costs $11,000, has a salvage value of $1000, and an estimated life of ten years. Using straight line depreciation, the accountant will deduct $1000 from income for each of the next ten years. The economist is not so much concerned with historic cost as capitalized earning capacity. Depreciation, or as economists often prefer, capital consumption allowances, should be based on market value or replacement costs. To calculate this, a better, but not perfect, way is to take a percentage of the value of the goods produced during a given period. In our example, let us say the capital costs in that industry were 10 percent of sales. Then, if in the third year the machine produced goods valued at $15,000, a deduction of $1500 would be taken. The wording here is ambiguous, but it

Constitutional Insight

the national government?
national government are th
of Article 1. The first 17 cl
are often called the nation
They confer on Congress
ranging from taxation a
armed forces of the v
district (Washingto
The 18th and
power to do w
ous list of p
lay and co
merce."
order

leans toward the economist's view since no limit is set on the amount one can deduct over the years.

A related problem is encountered in extractive industries. Accountants approach the problem by capitalizing all exploration costs.[28] They then set up a group of depletion accounts. As ore or whatever is removed, the depletion is calculated on a per unit basis. For example, suppose the exploration and start-up costs for a mine are $500,000. If the mine will produce 250,000 tons of ore, the cost per unit is $2 and will be recovered in the accounts as the ore is mined. If in the third year of operation 20,000 tons are extracted, the depletion allowance will be $40,000. Again, the economist would prefer to base the depletion allowance on the value of what the mine produces.

In the 1913 law all extractive industries were allowed to use 5 percent of the value of the product at the mine or well as a depletion figure. Depreciation was ultimately to come under the accountant's definition, but the rules for extractive industries were to follow a meandering course. Long and difficult political and administrative battles lay ahead in this area.

A deduction was also allowed for the amount received in dividends from corporations that themselves paid the normal tax.[29] In 1909, as part of the plan to kill the personal income tax, Congress had levied a corporation excise tax. Calculated on the basis of corporate income, with a $5000 exemption, it is hard to distinguish from an income tax. In any event, in 1913, as pointed out earlier, it was combined with the personal income tax with the rate set at the same level as the normal tax. Hence, it was felt that to subject dividends to the normal tax again would be double taxation. For normal tax purposes only, therefore, these dividends could be deducted.

The law tried to come to grips with the problem of taxpayers using holding companies to avoid the tax. This device involves a person setting up a corporation designed purely to hold stock—that is, a corporation having no operating functions whatever. The profits, the dividends from the stock, would then be allowed to accumulate for no reason other than avoiding the tax. The law's provision was as follows:

For the purpose of this additional tax the taxable income of any
individual shall embrace the share to which he would be entitled of
the gains and profits, if divided or distributed, whether divided or
distributed or not, of all corporations, joint-stock companies, or
associations however created or organized, formed or fraudulently
availed of for the purpose of preventing the imposition of such tax
through the medium of permitting such gains and profits to accumulate instead of being divided or distributed.

While the thrust of this section is clear, there are legal and administrative difficulties of the first order lurking here. The law requires intent to be present, attempting to separate such holding
companies from legitimate business enterprises which retain their
earnings for expansion. (A holding company could always be doc-
tored up with a few operating functions to try to make it seem as
legitimate as the next corporation.) How to implement such a provision? Cordell Hull and the law's other drafters provided that

the fact that any such corporation, joint-stock company, or association is a mere holding company, or that the gains and profits are
permitted to accumulate beyond the reasonable needs of the business shall be prima facie evidence of a fraudulent purpose to escape
such tax; but the fact that the gains and profits are in any case
permitted to accumulate and become surplus shall not be construed
as evidence of a purpose to escape the said tax in such case unless the
Secretary of the Treasury shall certify that in his opinion such
accumulation is unreasonable for the purposes of the business.

It was to be decided on a case by case basis then, with the commissioner empowered to levy the tax against the individuals who would
have gotten the income if distributed.

The rate structure was developed in such a way as to make
"stoppage at the source" easier. One of the main difficulties associated with an income tax has always been its administration. The
necessity for self-assessment opens the door to all manner of fraud
and evasion. The Civil War tax, for instance, had been plagued by
widespread abuse. Stoppage at the source, or deducting the tax
before money was given those subject to the tax, was seen as one
way to lessen the problem. However, combining this administrative
strategy with graduated rates presented a new difficulty. How was a

corporation to know, for instance, what bracket the recipients of its bond interest payments were in?

The ingenious solution was to have a flat rate "normal" tax to which everyone above the exemption was subject. Then beginning at a certain level, surtaxes could be imposed. This would give a net effect of progression throughout the rate structure, and, by providing that only the normal tax would be stopped at the source, ease the administrative burden.

The normal tax was set at 1 percent with the following surtaxes:

Percentage Rate	On Amounts Between
1	$ 20,000–50,000
2	50,000–75,000
3	75,000–100,000
4	100,000–250,000
5	250,000–500,000
6	Over 500,000

The exemption level was the subject of much debate, but there was little doubt that it would be set rather high. The figure selected was $3000 with $1000 more allowed for a married person (but with only one $4000 exemption allowed per couple).

Taken as a whole, the law received the blessing of most economists. They had some criticisms regarding specific provisions, but most felt that given the circumstances it was about as well thought out a measure as could be hoped for. Politically, it satisfied all but the most radical Democrats. The stage was now set for continual pressures for change and responses to those pressures.

NOTES

1. See Joseph Hill, "The Civil War Income Tax," *Quarterly Journal of Economics*, 8 (July, 1894), 416–52 and E.R.A. Seligman, *The Income Tax: A Study of the History, Theory and Practice of Income Taxation at Home and Abroad* (New York: Macmillan, 1914), Part II, Chap. 4.

2. See Sidney Ratner, *Taxation and Democracy in America* (New York: Wiley, 1967), 177–80.

3. *Pollock v. Farmers' Loan and Trust Company*, 157 U.S. 429 (1895) 158 U.S. 601 (1895).

4. See Seligman, *Income Tax*, Part II, Chap. 5 and Ratner, *Taxation*, Chap. 10.

5. Concurring opinion, 157 U.S. 429.

6. Henry Pringle, *The Life and Times of William Howard Taft* (New York: Farrar and Rinehart, 1939), Vol. I, 421–25.

7. See Kenneth Hechler, *Insurgency* (New York: Columbia University Press, 1940) and L. James Holt, *Congressional Insurgents and the Party System, 1900–1916* (Cambridge, Mass.: Harvard University Press, 1967).

8. Pringle, *Taft*, I, 433; Nathaniel Stephenson, *Nelson W. Aldrich* (New York: Scribners, 1930), 354–56; George Mowry, *Theodore Roosevelt and the Progressive Movement* (Madison: University of Wisconsin Press, 1946), 58; *New York Times*, June 15, 1909.

9. See John D. Beunker, "The Adoption of the Income Tax Amendment: A Case Study of a Progressive Reform," Unpublished Ph.D. dissertation, Georgetown University, 1964.

10. See Richard Goode, "The Economic Definition of Income," in Joseph A. Pechman, ed., *Comprehensive Income Taxation* (Washington: Brookings, 1977), 1–36; William W. Hewett, *The Definition of Income and Its Aplication in Federal Taxation* (Philadelphia: Westbrook, 1925); and Paul H. Woeller, "Concepts of Taxable Income," *Political Science Quarterly*, 53 (March and December, 1938), 83–110 and 557–83.

11. Henry Simons, *Personal Income Taxation* (Chicago: University of Chicago Press, 1938), 50. For an elaboration of Simons' views see Walter Hettich, "Henry Simons on Taxation and the Economic System," *National Tax Journal*, 32 (March, 1979), 1–9.

12. Robert M. Haig, "The Concept of Income: Economic and Legal Aspects," in Haig, ed., *The Federal Income Tax* (New York: Columbia University Press, 1921), 7.

13. The best study of this problem is Lawrence H. Seltzer, *The Nature*

and Tax Treatment of Capital Gains and Losses (New York: National Bureau of Economic Research, 1951).

14. The best discussion of the issues surrounding progressive taxation is Walter Blum and Harry Kalven, *The Uneasy Case for Progressive Taxation* (Chicago: University of Chicago Press, 1953).

15. See Charles O. Galvin and Boris I. Bittker, *The Income Tax: How Progressive Should It Be?* (Washington: American Enterprise Institute for Public Policy Research, 1969).

16. Of course, as the character of governmental expenditures has changed to include more social welfare spending this argument would seem to lose some of its cogency. However, some argue that welfare expenditures, too, are made to protect the wealthy by buying off political discontent. Frances Fox Piven and Richard Cloward, *Regulating the Poor: The Functions of Public Welfare* (New York: Pantheon Books, 1971).

17. *Congressional Record*, September 8, 1913.

18. Although its focus is on more recent events, David Walker, *Toward a Functioning Federalism* (Cambridge, Mass.: Winthrop, 1981), Chap. 6 contains a good overview of the issues.

19. I am drawing on the familiar work of David Easton, but only for heuristic purposes. *A Systems Analysis of Political Life* (New York: Wiley, 1965).

20. On the role of elites, see Robert Putnam, *The Comparative Study of Political Elites* (Englewood Cliffs, N.J.: Prentice-Hall, 1976).

21. Thomas Reese, "The Politics of Taxation," Unpublished Ph.D. dissertation, University of California at Berkeley, 1976, Chap. 2.

22. On Ways and Means' role in the House see Neil MacNeil, *Forge of Democracy* (New York: David McKay, 1963) and John Manley, *The Politics of Finance: The House Committee on Ways and Means* (Boston: Little, Brown, 1970). Both deal more with contemporary politics than its historical role, though.

23. *Congressional Record*, April 26, 1913.

24. Seligman, *Income Tax*, 682.

25. *Eisner v. Macomber*, 252 U.S. 189 (1920) and *Merchant's Loan and Trust Company v. Smietanka*, 255 U.S. 509 (1921).

26. U.S. *Statutes at Large*, 63rd Cong. 1st sess., Chap. 16, 167.

27. Art II, sec. 1; Art. III, sec. 1.

28. See Dixon Fagerberg, "Metal Mining Companies," in *Encyclopedia of Accounting Systems* (Englewood Cliffs, N.J.: Prentice-Hall, 1976), Vol. III, 1269–1310.

29. The rate structure of the 1913 law was set up in a rather unusual way. Taxpayers were subject to two taxes on their incomes. First, there was a "normal" tax which was a uniform percentage; then, there was a "surtax" which was graduated. This bifurcation was done for administrative reasons, as explained below.

II

The Revenue Act of 1916
and the War Revenue Act
of 1917

The Revenue Act of 1916

Less than a year after the enactment of the income tax, war had erupted in Europe. The initial effect of the hostilities was to send the American economy reeling. Exports to European countries all but came to a halt, the financial markets saw a dramatic fall in stock prices, a banking crisis quickly developed, imports fell sharply, and, as the economic uncertainty spread, industrial production declined, setting off another round of economic paralysis. The impact of all these factors on the federal revenue picture was staggering as receipts plummeted from $73,224,173 in July to $44,563,946 in October.[1]

By the summer of 1915, however, an economic turnabout was in the making. A banking collapse had been averted, stabilizing the monetary situation, and as the war lengthened, European orders for American goods began to pile up. Even so, the government's financial position did not improve. On the receipt side the low level of imports meant that customs duties, still the staple of the revenue structure, were markedly diminished. To make matters worse, the budget was further unbalanced by increased expenditures. The early reforms of the Wilson presidency had led to the creation of new administrative bodies and new expenditure objects.[2] Then, the ill-fated attempt to capture Pancho Villa resulted in another severe drain on the Treasury.

Nevertheless, by far the most important element in the financial equation was the movement toward "preparedness." As the European war dragged on, there was increasing agitation in the United States to begin an armament program. Although many Democrats opposed preparedness, Wilson moved to join this camp in late 1915. In his message to Congress in December of that year he advocated huge increases for national defense.[3]

Congress had reacted to the immediate fall in revenue with the Emergency Revenue Act of 1914, passed on October 22. It raised a number of excise taxes and levied several new ones, but did not contain any provision affecting the income tax. The act was designed as a temporary measure, scheduled to expire on December 31, 1915; however it was soon extended to December 31, 1916. With the escalating expenditures brought on by the preparedness program, though, this measure did not come close to balancing the books. By late 1915, therefore, it was obvious to key decision makers in public finance that a new revenue bill would have to be acted upon in the near future.[4]

President Wilson had only a passing interest in tax matters and leaned heavily on his Secretary of the Treasury William G. McAdoo.[5] He did have, though, strong feelings that the increased military expenditures should be financed through taxation rather than borrowing. Moreover, his generally progressive orientation made him favor use of the income tax rather than excises and increased customs. McAdoo was generally held to be knowledgeable in fiscal matters, but his major concern, like Wilson's, was that the books be balanced and borrowing held to an absolute minimum. It is fair to say also that both these men had an appreciation of the role of Congress in tax policy. They, through McAdoo, frequently offered suggestions, especially in the early stages of a bill, but they did not formulate a program and attempt to employ the executive branch's resources to push it through. Instead, they provided expenditure totals and more or less left it to the legislators to come up with the specifics.

In Congress the Democrats were in control of both houses, giving them the chairmanship of all committees and subcommittees. As noted earlier, the internal politics of Congress in those days were such that party solidarity was much more important than was the case later. It was customary for the majority party members of a committee to meet and thrash out their disagreements. Then when the full committee met, it was merely to ratify these agreements. The same rule held for conference committees. Further, the party caucuses in both houses had the power to order a binding vote. Sometimes, therefore, depending on the persons involved, a dispute within a committee might be taken to the caucus, where a decision was final.

The Democratic chairman of the House Ways and Means Committee was Claude Kitchin of North Carolina.[6] Charming, but passionately committed to his principles, he was the most powerful figure in the House since he also chaired the Democratic caucus. A tireless worker, he, true to James Madison's wishes, possessed a strong sensitivity about the role of the House, especially in revenue matters. Politically, he was almost a populist and a pacifist, a proponent of taxing the rich and an opponent of preparedness—and later of war. Though he was usually vilified by the urban press of the Northeast and pictured as something of an ignorant provincial, he had a solid grasp on both the technical and philosophical issues involved in revenue matters.

Chairing the important Subcommittee on Internal Taxation was Representative Cordell Hull.[7] Hull, like McAdoo, came from Tennessee, where he had been the political protege of Benton McMillan, the author of the 1894 income tax law. In 1913 Hull had been appointed to draw up the income tax amendment to the tariff and had guided it through the House. A serious student of foreign systems of taxation, he was the match of any expert. He possessed, further, a strong populist heritage and a distinct distrust of large corporate interests.

On the Senate side Furnifold M. Simmons, also of North

Carolina, sat in the chair of the Finance Committee.[8] An "old southern gentleman" type of politician, Simmons was steady rather than persuasive. He preferred to assume the role of an engineer of consensus, not that of a dynamic leader. On income tax matters he usually deferred to John Sharp Williams who headed the Subcommittee on Income and Estate Taxes.[9] A member of the populist wing of Mississippi's Democratic party, Williams had a genuine dislike for urban-oriented northern business interests. He believed that for years the poor had been paying far too much of the federal government's budget via the customs duties and that the income tax should be used as a balance wheel. Williams, too, was strongly opposed to preparedness, viewing it as a sop to the east coast and its arms contractors.

Lastly, passing notice must be given to Oscar Underwood.[10] He had, as a Representative from Alabama, chaired the Ways and Means Committee during the first two years of the Wilson presidency. He was sent to the Senate in 1914, and though offered a seat on finance, chose one on appropriations. Nevertheless, his was a respected voice on revenue matters.

Since the revenue bill was considered during the summer of 1916, the upcoming election was ever present. Both the White House and congressional Democrats, therefore, were always looking over their shoulders to see if what they were contemplating doing might have adverse electoral consequences.

In late November 1915 McAdoo began the political process by putting out some general ideas.[11] Wilson followed with a speech to Congress on December 7. McAdoo huddled with key Democrats from Congress soon afterwards to discuss specifics.[12] Kitchin, ever wary of leaning too heavily on the executive branch, asked Cordell Hull to spend the Christmas holidays in Washington drawing up the bill.[13] In January 1916 the Democrats on Ways and Means began meeting regularly on the bill. The omnibus character of this bill, of which the income tax was only a part, made it extremely complex. Accordingly, it was not until July 5 that it was reported to the House floor,[14] with passage coming five days later by a 240 to 140 margin.

The Senate Finance Committee kept the bill a month. Controversies kept spilling over to the Democratic caucus, delaying floor consideration until August 22.[15] The floor debate lasted off and on for three weeks, with a vote taken September 5 (42–16).

A conference committee was appointed immediately and reported two days later.[16] Its report was accepted easily, and Wilson soon signed the measure.

Raising the income tax rates was an almost universally backed solution to the fiscal crisis, in company with increases in most other taxes. This could be accomplished in several ways: by lowering the exemption, lowering the level at which the surtaxes began, uniformly increasing the normal and/or surtax rates, or increasing the graduation of the surtax scales.

McAdoo and Wilson only offered the most general comments. Wilson said in his December speech:

> To what sources, then, shall we turn? This is so peculiarly a question which the gentlemen of the House of Representatives are expected under the Constitution to propose an answer to that you will hardly expect me to do more than discuss it in very general terms. We should be following an almost universal example of modern governments if we were to draw the greater part or even the whole of the revenue we need from the income taxes. By somewhat lowering the present limits of exemption and the figure at which the surtax shall begin to be imposed and by increasing, step by step throughout the present graduation, the surtax itself, the income taxes as at present apportioned would yield sums sufficient to balance the books of the Treasury at the end of the fiscal year 1917 without anywhere making the burdens unreasonably or oppressively heavy.[17]

Soon thereafter the secretary of the treasury added some specifics, calling for a lowering of the exemptions to $2000 and $3000, beginning the surtaxes at $10,000 or $15,000 rather than $20,000, and increasing the rates themselves.[18] Kitchin and the Ways and Means Committee, however, came up with a different rate structure. They kept the exemption at the same level, but doubled the normal tax to 2 percent. The following were the proposed surtaxes:

Percentage Rate	On Amounts Between
1	$ 20,000–40,000
2	40,000–60,000
3	60,000–80,000
4	80,000–100,000
5	100,000–150,000
6	150,000–200,000
7	200,000–250,000
8	250,000–300,000
9	300,000–500,000
10	Over 500,000

One important exception was made in the coverage of the exemption, one which allowed the $4000 exemption to be used by any "head of a family" whether married or not.

On the floor more reform-oriented Democrats tried to argue that the surtax rates should be increased even more.[19] These proposals ran as high as 50 percent at the top brackets. Republicans, on the other hand, advocated lowering the exemption to $1500. Both sets of amendments were easily defeated.

The Senate Finance Committee kept the House surtax rates, except that they added further breakdowns above $500,000. They proposed 10 percent on the $500,000 to $1,000,000 bracket, 11 percent on the $1,000,000 to $1,500,000 bracket, 12 percent on the $1,500,000 to $2,000,000 bracket, and a top rate of 13 percent on all income over $2,000,000. While raising the rates in this manner sparked only moderate controversy, when a majority of one voted to lower the exemptions to $2000 and $3000, the losers appealed to the caucus.[20] Even though the extra $1000 subject to the tax was to be taxed at only 1 percent, many feared the electoral consequences of such a move. The caucus, after lengthy deliberation, overturned the committee and retained the previous exemption levels. The caucus did not overturn, however, the committee's decision to drop the "head-of-family" provision.

Some progressive senators, not satisfied with the rates, tried unsuccessfully on the floor to have them raised. Far more fireworks were touched off, though, by another attempt to lower the exemptions. Oscar Underwood threw his prestige behind a move to lower them to $2000 and $3000. The reason for this was not to raise additional revenue; rather, it was to "make better citizens" of the new taxpayers, and in so doing "to give stability and life and confidence to this great piece of legislation we are considering."[21] Despite his pleas, Underwood's proposal lost by a wide margin after he was roundly condemned by the Democratic leadership for even offering it.

A concerted effort was made to have the head-of-family exemption restored. Senator Williams said the committee took it out primarily because it penalized people who got married. Suppose, for example, a man is classified as head of a family and has an income of $3500. He has, under the House version, a $4000 exemption and pays no tax. He is thinking of marrying a woman with a $2500 income who now pays no tax because she falls under the $3000 exemption. If they get married, their joint exemption will be $4000, making $2000 of their income taxable.[22] Another inequity it would create would be a bonus for two related adults living together, say two sisters. One would be entitled to take a $4000 exemption and the other to take the single exemption.

A number of senators contended they still thought that at least widows and widowers ought to qualify for the higher exemptions. After several unsuccessful attempts to come up with language that suited Williams, the Senate voted down the idea.

When the bill went to conference, the rate and exemption questions were balanced between the houses. The Senate rates were kept while the higher exemption was extended to heads of families.

Soon after the 1913 act's passage a controversy had erupted over the taxability of stock dividends.[23] At times a corporation will distribute new shares of stock to its shareholders in place of cash dividends.[24] In these years, an accounting entry was made transferring some of the retained earnings to a capital stock account when this was done,[25] though neither the value of corporate assets nor the percentage holding of any stockholder changes. However, the earnings of the corporation have, in one sense (in that they are not available for cash dividends), been "distributed" and, since market value and book value are seldom the same, the stock dividend may represent substantial monetary value.

There are four ways to handle this problem: two by immediate taxation when received, two by postponing the tax until the stock is sold. If stock dividends are to be taxed as income on receipt, they can be taxed at either book or market value. On the other hand, if the gain at time of sale is taxed, what is the basis of the shares? They could be valued at zero or the original cost of the stock could be spread over the old and new shares.

The Ways and Means Committee explicitly enlarged the definition of income to say that dividends would include "any distribution made or odered to be made by a corporation out of its earnings or profits and payable to its shareholders, whether in cash or in stock of the corporation." On the floor, Representative Longworth, a Republican, suggested market rather than book value as the measure of income and Kitchin agreed to the amendment.[26]

Income, as had been defined under the 1913 statute, had included gains a person made in transactions not connected with his or her regular business. Examples would include such things as apartment buildings bought and sold by a doctor or the sale of shares of stock by a college professor. However, the commissioner had refused to allow losses in similar transactions to be deducted in arriving at net gain. Hence, an occasional stock speculator might emerge from the year with a loss but still have to pay taxes on all gains.

The Ways and Means Committee added a deduction for such losses but limited it to the extent of gains. The Senate committee kept this House provision, but on the Senate floor several senators pressed for deduction of all such losses.[27] Williams indicated he had some sympathy with this position, but added that the Treasury feared too much fraud would result if all losses were allowed. A lengthy discussion occurred over how the law might be worded to allow full deductibility but still prevent fraud. Finally, such a provision was adopted over Williams's objection. In the conference committee, though, Kitchin was adamant that it be returned to the House version, and Williams readily consented.

Another problem area involved the sticky subject of capital

gains. If income is an annual flow separate from capital, are appreciations in the value of capital goods income? Virtually all foreign statutes answered in the negative, meaning only goods bought and sold within the same year produce income (except, of course, for stock in trade). The American law, on the contrary, included such accretions to capital in income but postponed the levying of the tax until the time of sale.[28]

The Civil War income taxes had been ambiguous on this point, especially concerning gains on real estate transactions. The Revenue Act of 1870, last of that era's income taxes, had explicitly included gains from real estate acquired within two years of the sale date. The 1894 statute had copied this provision, but it was omitted in 1913. In the latter enactment all property was given the value it had on March 1, 1913, as a basis for any future sale.

Several members of the Senate Finance Committee wanted to return real estate to the special status it had earlier simply by restoring the two-year rule. There was considerable opposition to the proposal both in committee and on the floor. Nonetheless, the plan was carried in both forums. In the conference committee Kitchin wanted no more part of this than the full deductibility of losses, and the Senate conferees were forced to relent.

As noted earlier, one of the knottiest problems of business income taxation involves extractive industries. For coal and metallic industries the provisions of the 1913 law were working reasonably well. Oil, however, presented a more difficult problem. First, given the technology of the day, there was no way to know how much a well might produce when it began pumping. Second, when oil was struck, there was always a much heavier flow initially than during most of the well's life. In the parlance of the trade, these were called the "flush flow" and the "regular flow."

The Senate Finance Committee took up this thorny problem, about which Williams said there was "no part of this bill which has been more anxiously studied and which presented more difficulties than this part of it."[29] Senator Chilton, reputed to be an expert in the oil business, was relied on heavily. The oil men wanted to use the flush flow as the base for their depletion allowance, thereby allowing themselves more rapid write-off of drilling and lease costs. Chilton, however, convinced the committee that the regular flow was a more accurate measure. On the floor, several senators from oil-producing states objected, but the provision remained in with only a few dissenting votes. In conference, it was not a subject of controversy.

This first reform of the income tax is pretty much what one would expect, coming as it did soon after the initial law and with almost the same people in power as before. The rates were raised but not that dramatically, and both the normal and surtax rates were proportionally adjusted. No really radical changes were even entertained, and there appeared to be some genuine attempts to correct inequitable provisions by special amendments.

Keeping the level of surtax imposition at $20,000 was in line with Democratic ideology and electoral interests. The party of Jefferson appealed to few voters with $20,000 incomes anyway. Moreover, with an election two months away from the bill's passage, it is also not surprising that the exemption was not lowered.

The act did see, though, the first erosion of the tax base by giving exemptions to a number of people by virtue of their status. This had the dual effect of lowering the effective rates of taxation to which a number of people were subject and diminishing the Treasury's take of the national income. Such a move, while perhaps laudable, was to lead to, and make it harder to resist, demands for other exemptions because of status.

It is hard to quarrel with the allowing of loss deductibility in nonregular business transactions to the extent of gains. Indeed, E. R. A. Seligman had criticized this feature of the original law soon after it was enacted.[30]

Keeping real estate gains fully taxable may have risked a court battle, but it preserved an important feature of the American law. Such a provision as the one proposed would have left a convenient loophole for many (by such devices as fictitious sales). Obviously, too, the administrative burdens would have been enormous. Moreover, with its enactment would have come an avalanche of requests that other property be given the same status. Better that this dog lie for a while longer.

Unfortunately for conspiracy theories, nothing sinister appears to have been involved in the oil depletion allowance change. It seems to have been a genuine attempt to write a special provision into the law in order to make more general principles apply to a special business. What it did, however, was to use a *flow* for depletion allowance calculation. A door was therefore opened for the creation of a special part of the revenue code. In 1918 it was to swing widely open.

The act, it must be remembered, was designed primarily to raise revenue. Most probably hoped that the arms its proceeds were to buy would soon be set aside, allowing the rates to be lowered. The income tax, though, by this act proved itself to be one of the easiest taxes to juggle and was soon to be put to a greater test than was ever foreseen by those members of Congress who headed home to campaign in that autumn of 1916.

The War Revenue Act of 1917

As the United States inched toward active involvement in what was to become the "war to end all wars," projected expenditures for military hardware continued to run far ahead of receipts. By December 1916, Secretary McAdoo was sounding the alarm. He estimated that fiscal 1917 would see a deficit of $82,376,000, a figure which by 1918 would grow by another $282,471,000.[31] Without providing any specifics, he urged Congress to take immediate action.

In response, Congress enacted the Revenue Act of March 3, 1917. Although in its initial stages there had been some talk about raising income taxes, these ideas were omitted at the Ways and Means Committee stage. Instead, estate and excess profits taxes were scaled upward.[32] By the next month, however, the United States had declared war, and these measures were clearly inadequate. Congress and the Treasury now faced the huge task of tapping the booming economy for unprecedented revenues.

Political and economic complications abounded. First, the war had spurred economic activity but had not spread these benefits evenly. Huge profits were accumulating to many, but a soaring inflation was creating hardships in many other quarters. Hence, there were bound to be demands to both reach the pockets of those enriched by the war and to spare those whose budgets were stretched by rising food, shelter, and clothing prices.

Second, the debate over conscription occurred at the same time that the revenue measure was being considered. The taking of young men involuntarily and requiring them to give up their jobs (for $30 a month pay) and perhaps their lives were inevitably to affect the question of taking people's money. Why not a "conscription of wealth" or at the least a "conscription of income"? Early on, the American Committee on War Finance put this question out in a nationwide campaign.[33]

Moreover, as almost always occurs at the outbreak of a war, there was much concern about bipartisanship. Neither the Democratic nor Republican leaders wanted to appear openly partisan, at least at this stage.[34] Both the Ways and Means and Senate Finance Committees strove, therefore, to put together a bill which could secure the backing of both parties.

Initially, also, some decision had to be made concerning the ratio of bonds to taxes. Some economists and politicians favored raising all the money by taxation; others favored utilizing bonds for the greater percentage.[35] A general consensus seemed to develop around a 50–50 split. Throughout the early stages of the war, this arrangement continued to serve as a benchmark, even though the reasons for its choice remained unclear, and even though it was assailed by both those desiring more taxes and those wanting more borrowing.

Another complication was that the Treasury's estimates of revenue needs kept changing during the bill's consideration. McAdoo first said that $1,800,000,000 would be adequate. Then, on May 15 he revised that to $2,245,000,000.[36] Later in the summer, July 25, he reported that nearly $6,000,000,000 would be required.[37] The first revision occurred during the House floor debate and the second during the Senate Finance Committee's labors. While one can sympathize with the Treasury officials in those uncertain days, the effects of their changing estimates on delicate political compromises were shattering.

Lastly, this bill, more than most tax bills, became ensnared in institutional sensitivity. The Ways and Means Committee had put the bill together hurriedly, without any public hearings. The Senate Finance Committee decided to hold such hearings, which naturally delayed the bill and gave opponents of various sections time to organize and lobby senators. Further, the political complexion of the

Senate Finance Committee was different from that of Ways and Means. Senator Simmons had been somewhat more reluctant to raise taxes and thought borrowing a sounder course.[38] Henry Cabot Lodge also carried greater weight as an opponent of steep surtaxes than did any Republicans in the House. As a further complication, Robert LaFollette and a small group of diehard progressives were almost uncompromising in their demands for high taxes on large incomes. During the long delay between House passage and the senate committee's report, there were persistent rumors that the upper chamber's committee was making drastic revisions in the bill, something which piqued Kitchin and several other members of Ways and Means. The North Carolinian told reporters on June 11:

> The Constitution expressly gives to the House the exclusive jurisdiction to originate revenue bills. If the spirit of that provision is violated by the Senate in the manner reports indicated, and the bill is rewritten, whatever influence I have will be used to prevent holding a conference with the Senate.[39]

The income tax was, as before, embedded in an omnibus revenue bill. A complicated package containing war profits taxes, increased postal rates, increased tariffs, estate taxes, and excise taxes on almost every good and service imaginable, the bill had something that alienated or pleased every conceivable interest group in the country. Under normal circumstances, it could never have been passed—as all freely admitted—but this was war. Nevertheless, virtually every section of the bill was controversial, and the income tax frequently was part of bargains and compromises which affected other parts of the bill.

This bill began its life in an informal session of the Ways and Means Committee held the day after Wilson's speech requesting a declaration of war.[40] While everyone agreed speed was important, it took until October 1 for the bill to emerge from both houses. Ways and Means formed a five-man subcommittee of ranking members (three Democrats and two Republicans) to consult with McAdoo and write the bill. A prcarious bipartisanship was maintained and a report to the full committee made May 1. Eight days later the proposal, with almost no full committee changes, was introduced in the

House.[41] On May 11, the Senate Finance Committee opened hearings on the bill before it had passed the House. The House debated the bill steadily for two weks, voting its passage (329–76) May 23. After ten weeks of hearings, the Finance Committee of the Senate, unable to secure unanimous approval, reluctantly delayed its report. Finally, with a consensus still out of reach, a majority and minority report were transmitted on August 6.[42] The minority report was not from the ranking minority members, however, as they lined up behind the bill, but from the dissident progressives. The Senate debate lasted over a month, with a filibuster threatened at one point. On September 10, the Senate voted 69–4 for passage. Two days later a conference committee was appointed and reported September 29.[43] On October 1 the report was accepted.

From the very beginning it was assumed by everyone that the income tax rates would be raised. The overwhelming reason, of course, was that the progressive income tax is the ideal tax in terms of flexibility. But there were three other arguments which were advanced to support higher rates. One was that the rates should be set at such levels that the government would get a fair proportion of the war profits. Incomes, especially at the upper levels, were rising rapidly, and in the name of justice, it was argued that at least a portion of this "unnatural" increase should be taken. Secondly, it was contended that a conscription of manpower demanded a conscription of incomes. The American Committee on War Finance, for instance, proposed that surtaxes be set at 2½ percent for amounts between $5000 and $10,000 and at 10 percent for amounts between $10,000 and $100,000.[44] All amounts over $100,000 would be subject to 98 percent surtax rates, which when coupled with the 2 percent normal tax would stop all incomes at $100,000. And, lest it be thought all wealthy persons objected to this scheme, several members of Congress supplied telegrams from wealthy constituents urging very high (90 percent to 100 percent) taxation on incomes above certain levels, usually $100,000.[45] Thirdly, the income tax was a general and not a specific tax. This offered two advantages to politicians. First, they could defuse opposition from specific groups, especially those opposed to excise taxes, by substituting higher income taxes for these levies. On a more idealistic plane, the excise taxes, it was argued, would fall heavily on the lower classes, including many families of servicemen. Hence, the progressivity of the entire tax structure could be altered by raising income taxes and eliminating or keeping at a minimum the excise taxes.

While everyone voiced support for some increase, many felt that the increases should be small and have a minimum graduation. There were, of course, the usual cries of "confiscation" at the suggestion of extremely high rates. On a more serious note, it was argued that crippling taxation of high incomes would damage economic incentives for investment. A resulting moribund economy would do grave damage to the war effort. High taxation therefore might actually produce less revenue than more moderate rates. Similarly, it was noted that with steeply progressive rates high income persons would seek out tax-free state and municipal bonds, thus leaving the treasury depleted. It was shown several times during the debates that at a 12 percent marginal rate such bonds became the optimal investment. Thus, while there was a consensus for an increase in the rates, the nature and scope of that increase were quite controversial items.

Secretary McAdoo suggested leaving the normal tax at 2 percent but steeply increasing the surtax. His proposal was as follows:[46]

Percentage Rate	On Amounts Between
1	$ 3,000–4,000
2	4,000–5,000
5	5,000–10,000
7	10,000–20,000
8	20,000–40,000
10	40,000–60,000
12	60,000–80,000
15	80,000–100,000
20	100,000–150,000
25	150,000–200,000
33⅓	200,000–1,000,000
40	Over 1,000,000

The Ways and Means Committee adopted a somewhat different rate structure. Their bill set the normal tax at 2 percent for the first $2000 over the exemption and at 4 percent on the remainder. Their surtaxes were only slightly different:[47]

Percentage Rate	On Amounts Between
1	$ 5,000–7,500
2	7,500–10,000
3	10,000–12,500
4	12,500–15,000
5	15,000–20,000
6	20,000–40,000
8	40,000–50,000
11	60,000–80,000
14	80,000–100,000
17	100,000–150,000
20	150,000–200,000
24	200,000–250,000
27	250,000–300,000
30	300,000–500,000
33	Over 500,000

The effect was to raise the rates somewhat in the lower brackets, the result of doubling the normal rate, and to lower them in the higher brackets. Also, this version provided much smoother breakpoints and a more regular rise.

On the House floor, several progressive legislators tried to add amendments raising the surtaxes. Kitchin, though he probably personally approved of many of these, defended the committee bill and tried to maintain the bipartisan front he had labored to build. A movement was apparently growing, though, to increase the surtax levies by 25 percent and eliminate most of the rest of the bill. On May 17, Kitchin was forced to read a letter from Secretary McAdoo stating that more revenue was going to be needed.[48] The backers of higher surtaxes now had their chance and moved quickly. They successfully proposed to add 25 percent to each rate above $40,000 and to add a 45 percent bracket above $1,000,000.[49] Because of the new revenue picture, however, they could not couple this with a cut in excises. Known as the Lenroot amendment, its rates can be seen in the table reproduced below.

The Senate Finance Committee took out the House floor changes

Comparison of the House Rates and the Senate Finance Committee's Rates

	1916 Law	House Bill	Total	Senate Committee Bill	Total
	Percent	Percent	Percent	Percent	Percent
Normal rate	2	2	2	2	2
Additional tax rate on the amount of income in excess of					
$5,000 and not of $7,500	0	1	1	1	1
$7,500 and not of $10,000	0	2	2	2	2
$10,000 and not of $12,500	0	3	3	3	3
$12,500 and not of $15,000	0	4	4	4	4
$15,000 and not of $20,000	0	5	5	6	6
$20,000 and not of $40,000	1	6	7	8	9
$40,000 and not of $60,000	2	10	12	10	12
$60,000 and not of $80,000	3	13.75	16.75	12	15
$80,000 and not of $100,000	4	17.5	21.5	16	20
$100,000 and not of $150,000	5	20.25	25.25	20	25
$150,000 and not of $200,000	6	25	31	23	29
$200,000 and not of $250,000	7	30	37	26	33
$250,000 and not of $300,000	8	33.75	41.75	29	37
$300,000 and not of $500,000	9	37.5	46.5	31	40
$500,000 and not of $1,000,000	10	41.25	51.25	33	43
$1,000,000 and not of $1,500,000	11	45	56	33	44
$1,500,000 and not of $2,000,000	12	45	57	33	45
$2,000,000	13	45	58	33	46

Source: Senate Finance Committee, *Report to Accompany H.R. 4280*, 65th Cong., 1st sess. Senate Report #103.

and went back to the original Ways and Means bill. They did produce one alteration, though. They added 1 percent to all rates over
$15,000. The accompanying table, from the Finance Committee's
report, gives a comparative breakdown. (Note again that these surtaxes are in addition to those levied in the 1916 law.)

These figures were the result of delicate political balancing.
Senators Lodge and Penrose continually introduced amendments to
lower even further the surtaxes on incomes over $40,000. On the
other hand, LaFollette and others labored to keep the Lenroot
amendment, or preferably impose even more drastic rates. It was
only after McAdoo's second revised estimate in late July that the
extra 1 percent surtax was added, and even that hesitantly.

The progressives, led by LaFollette, refused to sign the report
and filed a strong dissent, ending the outward harmony. On the
floor, they offered a barrage of amendments to try to get higher
surtaxes put back in. They disapproved, they said, of borrowing and
thought taxes should be based strictly on ability to pay. After each
amendment was voted down, they modified it slightly and resub-
mitted it. Soon, they were picking up votes. Another senator offered
an amendent to create new brackets above $500,000. After this was
adopted, they offered the Lenroot amendment with the percentages
rounded off and managed to get enough votes to have it reinstated.

The Senate and House versions finally emerged, then, with
roughly the same rate structure. In the conference, this was a relatively easy part of the bill to deal with, the final rates being as
follows:

Percentage Rate	*On Amounts Between*
1	$ 5,000–7,500
2	7,500–10,000
3	10,000–12,500
4	12,500–15,000
5	15,000–20,000
7	20,000–40,000
10	40,000–60,000
14	60,000–80,000

18	80,000–100,000
22	80,000–100,000
25	150,000–200,000
30	200,000–250,000
34	250,000–300,000
37	300,000–500,000
40	500,000–750,000
45	750,000–1,000,000
50	Over 1,000,000

Turning to the allied question of the exemption levels, almost everyone also agreed that these should be lowered. The major argument again was revenue production. Opponents charged, though, that since the other taxes in the bill fell so heavily on low income persons, a high exemption was justified.

McAdoo proposed to lower the exemptions to $1500 for singles and $2000 for married persons and heads of households. In the subcommittee of Ways and Means this turned out to be a major issue. Not only was there controversy over whether to lower them this much, but also whether to lower both by the same amount. Some wanted to lower the one for marrieds and heads of households less than for single persons.[50] In the end, the subcommittee recommended $1000 and $2000, which was carried through the parent committee to the House floor. However, as noted above, a different rate of tax was proposed for the amount between the old exemption and the new one.

On the House floor several attempts were made to raise the exemption, but they all failed by wide margins. An amendment which commanded more serious attention was one based on the British practice of allowing an exemption for children.[51] Although voted down, it was reintroduced several more times, without any success.

When the bill moved to the Senate Finance Committee, the dollar amount of the exemption was retained but a provision was adopted that allowed the heads of families to deduct "$200 for each dependent child under 18 years of age or for each dependent child mentally or physically defective to such an extent as to be incapable of self-support. " On the Senate floor this provision was not attacked at all, but there was again concerted, albeit futile, effort to get the level of the exemption raised. In the conference committee, the House conferees agreed to allow the $200 per child exemption.

In the summer of 1917 several charitable organizations launched a campaign to have gifts to such bodies made exempt from both inheritance and income taxes. The Red Cross, for example, was conducting a massive campaign to raise $100,000,000 for war needs and urged that gifts to this effort be tax deductible.[52] A number of colleges sent letters to the Senate Finance Committee requesting such a move for themselves on a permanent basis.[53] The chairman of the Committee on War Charity and Social Work met personally with the Finance Committee to press for the idea.[54] Further, a number of resolutions from business groups also supported the move.[55] It was not put in the Finance Committee's bill, though. On the floor, instead, Senator Hollis offered it as an amendment, with a 20 percent of net income limitation. Senator Simmons, Finance chairman, agreed to accept it as a committee amendment if the limitation was reduced to 15 percent. Hollis consented, and it was then unanimously adopted.[56] In conference, it remained in without objection.

The change in individual tax rates enacted by the Revenue Act of 1916 had created a problem involving dividends. Dividends were taxable to the recipient as income, but the date at which the income was earned was unclear. Because dividends represent earned corporate income, should the income be recognized in the year it is earned or the year it is received (if there is a difference)? By the economists' definition of income it is clear that such income accrues in the year the corporation earns it. For tax administration purposes it is more convenient to have the tax liability accrue when the money is actually received. No problem existed as long as the rates remained stable; however, if year A's rate was 5 percent and year B's 10 percent, the year of recognition mattered.

By one view the corporation was a separate legal and taxpaying entity, and the corporation and individual income taxes were therefore entirely separable. The dividends, in consequence, would be payments to stockholders and taxed as income purely in the year of receipt. A contrary view held that the corporation was more or less an income-earning agent of the stockholders and that its income was theirs when earned. Dividends, then, well might represent income earned in previous years and, if so, ought to be taxed at that year's rates. Adopting the latter approach brings up the accounting problem of assigning a value to things drawn out of an unsegregated pool. The two simplest solutions to this problem are first in, first out and last in, first out. In this case, then, the dividends could be considered as either being paid out of the oldest or the most recent earnings, a decision which would clearly affect many persons' tax liability.

Congress opted for recognizing income when earned by the corporation and going for the last in, first out accounting method. That is, dividends were assumed to be paid out of the most recent corporate earnings, and if that caused a dip into a previous year's earnings, the income tax rates in effect then would prevail.

Stock dividends were once again a problem. Determining a fair market value for stock dividends, as required by the 1916 law, of corporate stocks not listed on stock exchanges had created vast administrative difficulties. Now, therefore, the taxable amount was changed to book value. This move did not placate stockholders generally, though, as they continued to claim that stock dividends should not be taxed at all.[57]

The Bureau of Internal Revenue had also found that the undistributed profits section of the 1916 statute was virtually unenforceable.[58] What that act did was to divide undistributed corporate profits, defined as those which "are permitted to accumulate beyond the reasonable needs of the business," among the stockholders as if they were distributed. The stockholders were then liable for the tax. The Senate Finance Committee discussed this problem and decided to try attacking it by placing a tax on the corporation that kept the undistributed profits. A tax of 10 percent was set on all earnings not "actually invested and employed in the business or . . . retained for employment in the reasonable requirements of the business" (or invested in U.S. bonds). It was hoped that this would serve as an incentive to distribute the earnings, but if, since most stockholders were in higher marginal brackets than 10 percent, it did not, some revenue would be forthcoming in any event.

From its inception this law was considered to be a temporary measure. The fact that the rates were merely added on to the 1916 ones indicates this as clearly as anything else. After the war's conclusion, the old rates would be restored. Nevertheless, the progressivity of the rates is surprising, as is the fact that McAdoo's and both committees' proposed rates were lower than those adopted. This was probably because the Democrats in the committees accepted compromises in this area to maintain a bipartisan front. On the floor, the ties of bipartisanship were loosened, and the progressives in both houses were determined to raise the surtax rates. While they did not get the extreme rates many wanted, they did succeed in giving the income tax, and hence the whole revenue measure, a more progressive cast.

Adding an exemption for children was another alteration in the exemptions given by virtue of status. Given the size of most families in 1917, this was a substantial exemption.

The decision to exempt charitable donations sounds plausible on its surface. Quite clearly, though, it represents a marked erosion of the tax base since most gifts come from persons of large means. Further, it is clear that the higher one's income, the more benefit one derives. At a 50 percent marginal rate the gift only costs half as much to the donor as the gift actually is. This may be seen as the first illustration of the principle that as tax rates rise, the wealthy will exert politicial pressure to have the way they spend their money create an exemption from taxation.

Furthermore, the provision created a sizeable interest group, or more properly interest groups, with a continuing interest in not tampering with a section of the revenue code. And since these are "sacred cow" type institutions, few politicians, no matter what their private sentiments, would vote against such a provision. Note that the Senate Finance Committee did not adopt the proposal, but when it was offered as a floor amendment, even its chairman recoiled from opposing it.

As for such matters as the timing of dividend earnings, the basis of stock dividends, and the undistributed profits provisions, they can be seen as the types of problems that were bound to occur with the law's implementation. The answers given in all the cases appear to have been reasonable efforts to grapple with these complexities.

The "temporariness" of this law, then, relates only to the rates. Decided in the heat of entering war, the act contained some major policy choices that were of a permanent character.

The revenue producing potential of the income tax was now appreciated by all knowledgeable persons. Without it, the task of raising revenue at this juncture in the nation's history would have been mind boggling. Roy Blakey wrote soon after the War Revenue Act of 1917 was on the books:

> The people of this country do not appreciate how fortunate, one might say how lucky, we are that our income tax law has been in force since 1913, so that we have had a little experience with it and some of the administrative machinery developed. . . . We are not at all certain how the machinery is going to stand the strain put upon it, but we shall be extremely interested observers and well wishers.[59]

NOTES

1. See Charles Gilbert, *American Financing of World War I* (Westport, Conn.: Greenwood Press, 1970), 14–26.

2. See Arthur S. Link, *Woodrow Wilson and the Progressive Era, 1910–1917* (New York: Harper and Row, 1954), Chaps. 2 and 3.

3. James D. Richardson, ed., and comp., *Messages and Papers of the Presidents*, Vol. XVII (New York: Bureau of National Literature, n.d.), 8102–8117.

4. Gilbert, *American Financing*, 26ff.

5. Biographical information on McAdoo can be found in John J. Broesamle, *William Gibbs McAdoo: A Passion for Change* (Port Washington, N.Y.: Kennikat Press, 1973) and Mary Synon, *McAdoo* (Indianapolis: Bobbs-Merrill, 1924). His autobiography *Crowded Years* (Boston: Houghton Mifflin, 1931) should also be consulted.

6. See Alex M. Arnett, *Claude Kitchin and the Wilson War Policies* (Boston: Little, Brown, 1937).

7. Hull's biographer is Harold Hinton, *Cordell Hull: A Biography* (Garden City, N.Y.: Doubleday, 1942). See also his *Memoirs of Cordell Hull* (New York: Macmillan, 1948), Vol. I.

8. See Richard L. Watson, "Furnifold M. Simmons," *North Carolina Historical Review*, 44 (Spring, 1967), 166–85 and J. Fred Rippy, ed., *F. M. Simmons: Statesman of the New South* (Durham: Duke University Press, 1936).

9. On Williams consult George C. Osborn, *John Sharp Williams: Planter-Statesman of the Deep South* (Baton Rouge: Louisiana State University Press, 1943).

10. See Evans C. Johnson, *Oscar W. Underwood: A Political Biography* (Baton Rouge: Louisiana State University Press, 1980).

11. *Washington Post*, November 26, 1915.

12. Broesamle, *McAdoo*, 157.

13. Hinton, *Hull*, 151–53.

14. U.S. Congress, House, Ways and Means Committee, *Report to Accompany H.R. 16763*, 64th Cong., 1st sess., House Report No. 922.

15. U.S. Congress, Senate, Finance Committee, *Report to Accompany H.R. 16763*, 64th Cong., 1st sess., Senate Report No. 793.

16. U.S. Congress, *Conference Committee Report to Accompany H.R. 16763*, 64th Cong., 1st sess., House Report No. 1200.

17. Richardson, *Messages and Papers*, 8113.

18. U.S. Department of the Treasury, *Annual Report for 1915*.

19. *Congressional Record*, July 7, 1916.

20. *New York Times*, August 12, 1916, and August 13, 1916.

21. *Congressional Record*, August 26, 1916.

22. Williams's logic is not airtight here for this problem occurs with the general marital exemption as well.

23. See the review in E.R.A. Seligman, "Are Stock Dividends Income?" *American Economic Review*, 9 (September, 1919), 517–36.

24. Its reasons for doing this could be any one of several. It may be short of cash because of economic adversity or because large sums are being poured into expansion or plant replacement.

25. For those unschooled in accounting, it must be stressed that "retained earnings" do not represent cash. When income is earned, it usually is represented by cash or receivables. However, these may be converted into other assets or used to reduce liabilities with no effect on the income accounts. At year's end the income account is closed into (transferred to) retained earnings by an entry. The accumulation of earnings, therefore, which a retained earnings account represents bears no relation to the corporation's cash position.

It should be noted that current accounting practice prefers a memorandum entry when stock dividends are paid out, a notation which does not affect the account balances.

26. Longworth, a member of Ways and Means, had agreed to speak in favor of the bill. Agreeing to this amendment may have been part of the bargain he struck with Kitchin.

27. *Congressional Record*, August 26, 1916.

28. For a thorough discussion see Lawrence Seltzer, *The Nature and Tax Treatment of Capital Gains and Losses* (New York: National Bureau of Economic Research, 1951), esp. Chaps. 1, 2, and 4.

29. *Congressional Record*, August 28, 1916.

30. E. R. A. Seligman, "The Income Tax of 1913," Appendix to his *The Income Tax: A Study of the History, Theory, and Practice of Income Taxation at Home and Abroad* (New York: Macmillan, 1914), 681.

31. U.S. Department of the Treasury, *Annual Report for 1916*, 45 and 47–48.

32. See Gilbert, *American Financing*, 80–82.

33. See the full page ad in the *New York Times*, April 1, 1917.

34. On the nonpartisanship of this period, see Seward Livermore, *Politics is Adjourned: Woodrow Wilson and the War Congress* (Middletown, Conn.: Wesleyan University Press, 1966).

35. For a survey of the economic arguments, along with citations to the literature of the period, see Gilbert, *American Financing*, Chap. 1.

36. The letter is reprinted in the *Congressional Record*, May 17, 1917.

37. This letter is reprinted in U.S. Congress, Senate, Finance Commit-

tee, *Report to Accompany H.R. 4280*, 65th Cong., 1st sess., Senate Report No. 103.

38. T. S. Adams, "Customary War Finances," *New Republic*, 10 (April 17, 1917), 292.

39. *New York Times*, June 11, 1917.

40. *New York Times*, April 4, 1917.

41. U.S. Congress, House, Ways and Means Committee, *Report to Accompany H.R. 4280*, 65th Cong., 1st sess., House Report No. 45.

42. Senate Finance Committee, Report No. 103, parts 1 and 2.

43. U.S. Congress, *Conference Report to Accompany H.R. 4280*, 65th Cong., 1st sess., House Report No. 172.

44. "The Conscription of Wealth," *Independent*, 90 (April 29, 1917), 193.

45. *Congressional Record*, May 15, 1917.

46. *New York Times*, April 16, 1917.

47. It must be noted that these surtax rates were to apply in addition to those levied by the 1916 law, whereas McAdoo's were not.

48. *Congressional Record*, May 17, 1917.

49. *Ibid.*

50. *New York Times*, April 27, 1917.

51. *Congressional Record*, May 15, 1917.

52. *New York Times*, June 18, 1917.

53. *New York Times*, June 24, 1917.

54. *New York Times*, June 23, 1917.

55. *New York Times*, June 8, 1917.

56. *Congressional Record*, September 7, 1917.

57. See the testimony of Paul D. Cravath of Bethlehem Steel Corporation, U.S. Congress, Senate, Finance Committee, *Hearings and Briefs before the Committee on Finance on H.R. 4280*, 65th Cong., 1st sess., May 11, 1917.

58. *Congressional Record*, August 20, 1917.

59. Roy G. Blakey, "The War Revenue Act of 1917," *American Economic Review*, 7 (December 1917), 810.

III

The Revenue Act of 1918

WHEN THE UNITED STATES declared war in 1917, there was little appreciation of the enormity of the enterprise they had undertaken. With typical American ingenuity, many of the logistical problems—the raising and training of an army, the operation of a nationwide rail system, the establishment of price controls, the movement of troops and supplies to France—were quickly overcome. Finance, however, always remains a constant, the income and outgo yielding to no amount of ingenuity, Yankee or otherwise.

Outlays for the military services continued to rise, with the totals made higher than necessary by the rapidity with which many contracts were signed without adequate cost controls. Many, in fact, were given on a cost-plus basis, which obviously was an open invitation to escalation of charges. Furthermore, the U.S. discovered that the Allies were in a much more desperate plight than had been thought, a situation which led to the advancing of large loans. By the early spring of 1918 Treasury forecasters were putting fiscal 1919 expenditures at $24,000,000,000.[1] Revenue to be taken in under the War Revenue Act of 1917 was estimated to run slightly over $4,000,000,000. Moreover, sales of Liberty Bonds, now in the third major campaign, were sluggish. From these figures Secretary McAdoo drew the grim conclusion that a new revenue bill was essential. At least one-third, already down from one-half, of the expenditures, he felt, must be raised by taxes.[2]

When word of McAdoo's intentions reached Congress, key Democrats rushed to register a strong protest.[3] Congress had hoped to adjourn by July 1, to leave Washington's heat and humidity to take to the campaign circuit. Too, Democratic leaders, sensing the party was in trouble, did not want the albatross of new taxes before November. They had already lost a special senatorial election in Wisconsin in April, even with the president's full backing.[4] One Ways and Means Democrat offered the view that not one Democratic seat in the North would be safe if a tax bill were passed. They urged the sale of more bonds to tide the Treasury over until after November and then have Wilson call a special session.

McAdoo, however, persisted. On May 8 he wrote to Wilson:

> Nothing is more imperative than new revenue legislation at this session of the Congress. . . . The War and Navy Departments and the Shipping Board have been changing their estimates. . . . Unless this matter is dealt with now firmly and satisfactorily, we shall invite disaster in 1919. I think it will be necessary for you, at the proper time, to deliver a special message to the Congress on the question of new revenue legislation.[5]

Cordell Hull, the lone Congressional dissenter, wrote Wilson on May 16 also urging that Congress be kept in session.[6]

On May 21 McAdoo met with Kitchin, Simmons, and the heads of both appropriations committees.[7] An ensuing stalemate produced a decision to put the matter to Wilson and accept his judgment. McAdoo immediately drafted a strong letter to Wilson and met with him the following day.[8] On the day after this, Wilson met for three hours with the Congressmen, after which the solons believed he had accepted their position.[9] On May 25 the president announced he would consent to a special postelection session if both parties would agree to passing a revenue act by January 1. Both the parties on Ways and Means quickly concurred, but the Republicans on Finance would not come around.[10] Now determined, Wilson decided to take his case directly to Congress, and, by implication, to the people. On May 27 he gave what most observers said was his best speech ever.[11] It was prepared hastily and caught most members of Congress by surprise (it was announced at 10:00 that he would speak at 1:00). But with news of a smashing Allied offensive reaching him just before he left the White House, his mood and moral tone—optimistic, firm, but not yet preachy—was at its best. He put the

case well for more revenue, but added as an aside that in his view the
"present tax laws are marred . . . by inequalities which ought to be
remedied." This gave every interest in the country a line to quote
(which almost every one of them did in the hearings). At the same
time he also intoned Congress to "care nothing at all for what is
being said and believed in the lobbies of Washington hotels," which
had filled in anticipation of a new tax bill. As an obvious reference to
the elections he said this duty must be met "without selfishness or
fear of consequences. Poltiics is adjourned." The next day, a cha-
grined Kitchin, who had wanted a revenue bill much earlier in the
session, merely said the commander-in-chief had spoken and that
deliberations would begin the following day.[12]

The Ways and Means Committee, or a quorum thereof, sat
throughout the summer conducting hearings with an exasperated
McAdoo trying to speed them up.[13] They reported to the House on
September 6, and fourteen days later the lower chamber approved
their bill unanimously. The State Finance Committee began hearings September 6 and reported to the Senate December 6. Passage
came here on December 23. The conference committee reached
agreement on February 6, 1919, with both houses concurring
shortly.

As with the two previous wartime revenue laws, the consideration of this one was accompanied by numerous political complications and nuances. For one thing both Kitchin and McAdoo
were in failing health. Kitchin was beginning to feel the effects of the
heavy wartime strain. Three years later, he was to become totally
inacapcitated.[14] McAdoo was stricken in the early summer while on
a Liberty Bond tour and spent most of his time in a hospital. Ultimately this illness forced him to resign on November 14, and he was
replaced by Carter Glass on December 16.[15]

Kitchin and McAdoo also unfortunately had their relations
strained. Kitchin had wanted a tax bill earlier in the session, but
McAdoo had not seen the necessity for one. When McAdoo began in
the spring to insist on a revenue bill, Kitchin felt betrayed. He
shortly thereafter accused McAdoo, in an indirect way, of being
unduly influenced by the publishers' lobby, who wanted to end the
postal zone system.[16] McAdoo angrily denied the allegation and de-

manded the evidence.[17] Kitchin shoved the whole matter aside, but ill feeling lingered. The sniping continued as McAdoo's patience wore thin with the length of Ways and Means's deliberations. Kitchin, meanwhile, felt McAdoo was not sensitive enough to the delicate maneuvering required to appear nonpartisan in a twenty-three member body. The secretary wired the president on July 25 that if the revenue bill were delayed, it would seriously hamper the sale of Liberty Bonds. Would Wilson "ask" Mr. Kitchin to finish it as soon as possible and "expedite its passage over other measures."[18] Wilson gave the telegram to Kitchin, who wired McAdoo acidly that "Every effort is being made to this end."[19]

The country's economy was continuing its strong performance. However, there was apprehension over the surging inflation in spite of selected price controls and the slowdown in Liberty Bond purchases.[20] There was also the beginning of talk about what economic conditions would be like when peace came. As the summer of 1918 wore on and peace appeared nearer, the public debate on this question became more widespread.

One of the most important events affecting the revenue bill was the war's end itself. The Armistice on November 11, while the bill was in the hands of the Senate Finance Committee, triggered an immediate reassessment of fiscal needs and conditions. Three days after this memorable event, McAdoo revised the estimates for 1919 to $18,000,000,000.[21] Applying the ratio of one-third, the total tax bill could now be scaled down to $6,000,000,000.

As in 1916, the approaching elections were leering over everyone's shoulder. It was difficult, for instance, to keep a quorum in place, especially by the Finance Committee. How to double taxes without inflicting undue political pain gave the Democrats plenty to think and ponder about. In general, the news from the country was not good for Democrats. Moreover, Wilson had cast an unusual tenor to the fall elections with his "politics is adjourned" statement in the spring. It hampered Democratic strategists in that they could not conduct an offensive against the Republicans. It left the Republicans a good bit of maneuvering room, however, for they could attack specific agencies or individuals while avoiding a frontal assault on Wilson. Ultimately this strategy baited Wilson into his blunderous announcement of October 25 requesting a Democratic Congress.[22] Now the opposition could feign shock and surprise that the president was violating his own admonition, while at the same time broadening the attack on all fronts. The timing of the statement furthermore allowed the Republicans plenty of time to make shrill charges but gave the Democrats no time to reply.

One of the issues Republicans had been playing up before the ill-fated announcement was the incompetency of many of Wilson's underlings. Since early in the war several Republican congressional leaders had been trying to set up a committee to "help" the president administer the war effort. Remembering the grief caused Lincoln by a similar committee, Wilson fought it strenuously. Although stifled in general, those who sought to embarrass the administration were able to use standing committees to air specific charges. Because Wilson's relations with several Democratic chairmen were not particularly amiable, they sometimes cooperated in these ventures. One which especially stung Wilson was an investigation by the Senate Military Affairs Committee which uncovered gross incompetency in aircraft procurement.[23]

These peripheral matters were important in the tax bill's consideration because they were evidence of a strained relation between Wilson and the Senate. His leaders there were for the most part lackluster men who could not hold even the Democrats in line. Moreover, Wilson's open dislike for several southern senators because of their opposition to the war (especially Hartwick and Vardaman) and his barely concealed desire to see them defeated in 1918 poisoned his relations further with several important Democrats. Naturally, much of this refracted onto McAdoo and other administration people.

After the voters' verdict in November, with the revenue bill still not through the legislative maze, there were further complications. McAdoo and Simmons wanted to go ahead and set the rates for 1920, arguing that "people need to know what they were going to have to pay."[24] The Republicans naturally saw little wisdom in this, preferring to wait "until economic conditions were known"—and until they controlled both tax writing committees.[25]

In addition, there were more than the usual number of attempts to attach riders to the revenue bill. First, as a reaction to *Hammer v. Dagenhart*, 247 U.S. 251 (1918), there was an amendment offered to tax companies employing child labor. Then there was the "Reed amendment" to make the District of Columbia "bone dry." Next, there was an early attempt to control corruption in campaigns by attaching a tax on all campaign contributions over $500. Lastly, there was a movement to give all returning soldiers and sailors a bonus. Each of these was adopted in some form at one place or another, and while only the last (in its final form) affected the income tax directly, they did bog down the bill by making the compromising and dealing more delicate than ever.

During the Finance Committee's deliberations the Eighteenth Amendment was ratified. This meant a heavy reduction in proposed revenue from alcoholic beverage taxes and necessitated the juggling of the others' rates.

To a degree greater than normal, agencies other than the Treasury entered the policy-making process. The secretary of the navy, for example, sought to influence the tax credit for military personnel.[26] The fuel administrator and two of his subordinates testified at length before congressional committees, with an attorney in this agency drafting an important amendment (ultimately adopted). The secretary of war was called to testify also, to give his opinions concerning estimated expenditures.

The fact that the income tax's rates had risen so dramatically at the last session altered the nature of its politics. When the top rate was 6 percent, even though the wealthy might dislike the tax, spending too much effort fighting it was not worth the cost. However, as the rates climbed, every dollar of additional income meant a much larger tax bite. Hence, for business income especially, how income and deductions were treated became vastly more important. Naturally, therefore, many more interests sought to influence the law. Several industry representatives before both committees said that "we didn't mind this provision when tax rates were low, but now. . . ." It was this act which saw major industries turn their attention away from excise taxes and concentrate on income taxes. As the former diminished in importance, their attraction was to the new main show. In the process, income tax politics were now to take on more and more the character of previous tariff and excise tax politics. Rather than defining the political format in terms of bargaining over the rates on this or that product, though, it was now a matter of bargaining over how income or deductions are computed in this or that line of business.

Lastly, some weight must be given to the conditions under which the two committees worked. The hot, humid Washington summer, capping an already long and grueling congressional session, made tempers short and nerves frayed. Moreover, with members in and out of the capital, bargains struck one day might be undone the next. The constant tempest of Wilsonian foreign policy, heightened as the war neared its end, only added to the general buzz of activity and the tension. All in all, it was probably the worst of times to consider the largest revenue bill in human history up to that point.

As always, setting the rates was a delicate task, compounded by the fact that they were going to levels absolutely unthinkable only five years before. There appeared to be genuine concern that the practical limit was close to being reached.[27]

Initially, however, the question of whether or not to draw a differential between earned and unearned income received a good bit of attention. McAdoo pushed this idea from the very beginning, and he had a powerful ally on Ways and Means in Representative Nicholas Longworth, a Republican from Ohio, who had been advocating this for years. Exactly why McAdoo wanted this so badly is not clear. It may have been tied to his concern about Liberty Bond sales, though, because he indicated that he thought they should be exempt from the differential.[28] Specifically, he advocated doubling the normal tax to 12 percent and tacking on a 3 percent differential for unearned income.

Longworth had given the matter more sustained thought and had studied the British statute, which did make such a distinction. His reasoning was that income from dividends, interest, and rent leaves one's capital intact, whereas when one uses himself to earn the income his capital is diminished. (That as a blanket assertion there are problems with this logic is obvious.) At the Ways and Means hearing he grilled Treasury people on whether such a policy could be administered. Although they admitted it would introduce many complexities, they thought it could be done.

Kitchin, on the other hand, did not like the idea, arguing that the definitions would be too difficult to write. On August 16, though, on a very close vote the committee overruled its chairman and inserted the provision.[29] Four days later Kitchin asked the Treasury to work out the details for its administration.[30] On the 26th he met with McAdoo over the whole question of rates, a cool meeting which ended without agreement.[31] To the president they both went once again. Meanwhile the Treasury people admitted they were having difficulty setting up the specifics. Ways and Means then reversed itself and inserted the following statement in its report:

> The committee gave careful consideration to the advisability of making a differential between earned and unearned income, but finally determined that a flat normal tax was advisable in view of the difficulty experienced by the committee in finding a satisfactory method of distinguishing between earned and unearned income (a difficulty also experienced by the Treasury Department) and in view of the almost insuperable difficulties in the administration of such a differential and the added complications in the law which would be necessitated thereby. The Treasury Department also gave careful consideration to this question and reached the same conclusion as the committee.[32]

Thus, the controversial idea was dead for another session.

Raising the normal tax was a near unanimous policy choice for increasing the revenue to the desired levels. The range discussed on Ways and Means was from 5 percent to 20 percent, with 12 percent settled on as the final figure. However, this was held to be a very high tax on those only slightly above the exemption (most of whom were probably Democratic voters). Hence, it was decided to halve the rate applying to the amount between the exemption and $6000. Since the surtaxes began at $5000, what this did in effect was to merge the normal and surtaxes into an overall progressive rate. In the Senate Finance Committee this rate structure was left unmolested until the end of the war. At that point, they kept the idea of a two-tiered normal tax but reduced the percentages by one-third.[33]

The surtaxes were not as hot a topic of debate as usual. As can be seen in the accompanying table, the House version contained some rather rough jolts in its climb. In its turn the Finance Committee merely smoothed them out. On the floor LaFollette offered his usual amendment raising the rates, but the committee's version was adopted without further protest.[34] In conference no one seemed to object to the rate structure at all.

There were two categories of income-related questions raised in this tax bill. The first group encompassed the soldiers' bonus and some technical, but nonetheless important, questions. The second was the exclusion allowed to presidents' and judges' salaries, state officials' salaries, and interest from state and local bonds.

Amounts received by workers under state workmen's compensation statutes had been ruled by the commissioner to be nontaxable. Concurring in this judgment and not wishing it to be overturned later, the Ways and Means Committee wrote the exclusion into the law.

The exchange of property by two individuals creates an interesting tax situation. It can be argued that there should be no tax levied, since presumably if an exchange were made the values were equal. The new property would then merely assume the basis of the old and a gain not be recognized until a cash sale is made. Theoretically, however, this invalidates the principle that taxable gains ought to occur when a transaction is made. The other alternative, therefore, is to establish fair market value for the new property and recognize the gain over the adjusted basis of the old (cost plus improvements less depreciation) in the same way as if cash had been paid. The major problems with the second approach, which is much sounder in theory, are the administrative burdens it creates and the question it raises concerning the treatment of losses. The difficulty with the first is that it opens the door to all sorts of sham exchanges. Say a husband and wife each own an apartment building. One produces $10,000 in net rents; the other $100,000. In a year in which the husband's income from other activities is low, they can arrange an exchange and he report the $100,000—taxed, of course, at lower rates. If in the following year the wife's income is lower, they can exchange again, with her now able to pay the lower rates on the

House and Senate Surtax Rates in 1918

Surtax bracket upon the amount of the net income in excess of	Rate House	Rate Senate
$5,000 and not in excess of $6,000	2	1
$6,000 and not in excess of $7,500	2	2
$7,500 and not in excess of $8,000	3	2
$8,000 and not in excess of $10,000	3	3
$10,000 and not in excess of $12,000	7	4
$12,000 and not in excess of $14,000	7	6
$14,000 and not in excess of $15,000	7	6
$15,000 and not in excess of $16,000	10	6
$16,000 and not in excess of $18,000	10	7
$18,000 and not in excess of $20,000	10	8
$20,000 and not in excess of $22,000	15	9
$22,000 and not in excess of $24,000	15	10
$24,000 and not in excess of $26,000	15	11
$26,000 and not in excess of $28,000	15	12
$28,000 and not in excess of $30,000	15	13
$30,000 and not in excess of $32,000	20	14
$32,000 and not in excess of $34,000	20	15
$34,000 and not in excess of $36,000	20	16
$36,000 and not in excess of $38,000	20	17
$38,000 and not in excess of $40,000	20	18
$40,000 and not in excess of $42,000	25	19
$42,000 and not in excess of $44,000	25	20
$44,000 and not in excess of $46,000	25	21
$46,000 and not in excess of $48,000	25	22
$48,000 and not in excess of $50,000	25	23
$50,000 and not in excess of $52,000	32	25
$52,000 and not in excess of $54,000	32	26
$54,000 and not in excess of $56,000	32	26
$56,000 and not in excess of $58,000	32	27
$58,000 and not in excess of $60,000	32	28
$60,000 and not in excess of $62,000	38	29
$62,000 and not in excess of $64,000	38	30
$64,000 and not in excess of $66,000	38	31

House and Senate Surtax Rates in 1918 (Cont'd)

Surtax bracket upon the amount of the net income in excess of	Rate House	Rate Senate
$66,000 and not in excess of $68,000	38	32
$68,000 and not in excess of $70,000	38	33
$70,000 and not in excess of $72,000	42	34
$72,000 and not in excess of $74,000	42	35
$74,000 and not in excess of $76,000	42	36
$76,000 and not in excess of $78,000	42	37
$78,000 and not in excess of $80,000	42	38
$80,000 and not in excess of $82,000	46	39
$82,000 and not in excess of $84,000	46	40
$84,000 and not in excess of $86,000	46	41
$86,000 and not in excess of $88,000	46	42
$88,000 and not in excess of $90,000	46	43
$90,000 and not in excess of $92,000	48	44
$92,000 and not in excess of $94,000	48	45
$94,000 and not in excess of $96,000	48	46
$96,000 and not in excess of $98,000	48	47
$98,000 and not in excess of $100,000	48	48
$100,000 and not in excess of $150,000	50	52
$150,000 and not in excess of $200,000	50	56
$200,000 and not in excess of $300,000	52	60
$300,000 and not in excess of $500,000	54	63
$500,000 and not in excess of $1,000,000	58	64
$1,000,000 and not in excess of $5,000,000	60	65
$5,000,000	65	65

Source: *Congressional Record*, Senate, February 13, 1919.

$100,000. The Ways and Means Committee opted for the first approach but the Finance Committee for the second. In conference the senators prevailed.

The problem of when dividends were to be taxed also came up again. Ways and Means changed the 1917 rule to say that dividends were taxable to the recipient in the year they were received.[35] Although the Senate Finance Committee heard from businesses which said this was unfair, it left the new rule in place. Corporations, for instance, who had one big project, say a bridge, may incur expenses for several years and use any revenue to cover these. Then their dividends will come all at once; equity demanded, they argued, that the earnings should be spread over the years of construction. For other businesses, though, especially those with swollen war profits earned when the rates were high, this was a boon. They could now hold them until 1919 or 1920 when the rates would surely be lower and distribute them then. (They would perhaps have to pay the undistributed profits tax, but this was in most cases lower than the stockholders' marginal surtax rates.)

Lastly, under this rubric was the soldiers' bonus question. The first proposal was to merely pay them; but the Treasury said that was beyond its means. Hence, the proponents of this idea then sought to juggle the tax system to accomplish the same thing. Just as several questions—how much? to whom? a uniform amount or not?—would have to have been addressed if the payout scheme had been adopted, so now there were equally knotty problems with the tax juggle. The basic idea was to exempt servicemen from paying a portion of their taxes. Should it be limited to those serving in combat zones, or should all personnel on active service be covered? Should it cover only military pay, or should it cover other income? The final decision was to give an exclusion of up to $3500 of government pay for all in active service.

One of the greatest controversies attending this revenue bill swirled around the taxing of the interest on state and local bonds.[36] Legally, supporters of imposing the tax advanced three major arguments. The first was that the Sixteenth Amendment gave Congress the power to tax incomes "from whatever source derived." The amendment therefore allowed Congress to tax an individual's income, and levying such a tax was in no way a tax on a state or its instrumentalities. Second was the assertion that the major power given the national government by the Constitution was national defense. Since the states entrusted this duty to the national government, the overriding need now was for revenue to fulfil that purpose. Hence, no state could object to the national government carrying out its primary purpose. As a third line of defense some admitted their constitutional doubts but said that the function of Congress was not to decide such questions. This judgment should be left to the courts. On practical grounds, two additional arguments were advanced. One was that the exemption was hurting the sale of Liberty Bonds. The other, and probably most relevant, was that wealthy people were escaping taxation through this mechanism.

All these arguments were answered by compelling briefs from the other side. Legally, the main argument began with generous quotations from *McCulloch v. Maryland*, 4 Wheat 316 (1819). The very nature of our federal system was established by this case, insulating the two layers of government from infringing on each other's powers through the medium of taxation. *Van Brocklin v. Tennessee*, 117 U.S. 151 (1886), a case in which Tennessee was told it could not tax federal property, made the holding explicit as it relates to the states. Two parts of *Pollock v. Farmers' Loan and Trust*, 158 U.S. 601 (1895), were also relevant here. One was that even the dissenters had agreed that Congress had no power to tax state instrumentalities. The other, and more important, was that the decision did not hold the income tax per se unconstitutional, but only its nonapportionment among the states. In that light, the Sixteenth Amendment did not in any way expand the taxing power of Congress. It merely cancelled the apportionment requirement for income taxes. In *Peck v. Lowe*, 247 U.S. 165 (1918), the Supreme Court had given sanction to this view. The Sixteenth Amendment, it held, "does not extend the taxing power to new or excepted subjects, but merely removes all occasion which otherwise might exist, for an apportionment among the States of taxes laid on income, whether it be derived from one source or another." Therefore the Sixteenth Amendment had changed nothing of substance, and the old court cases were still controlling.

Furthermore, during the debate over ratification of the Sixteenth Amendment this question had been dealt with. Governor Hughes of New York had expressed his concern to the legislature. In response, Senator Elihu Root wrote him a lengthy letter saying that the amendment gave no such power to Congress. Likewise, Senator Borah, one of the key backers of the amendment, opined in 1910 that state and local bond interest would be immune from income taxation. Since the states ratified the amendment with this understanding, it would be undermining the nature of our government to now levy such a tax.

Turning to the practicalities, it was obvious that if the tax were levied, states and municipalities would have to raise the rates of interest on their bonds in order to attract buyers. This would necessitate, in most cases, raising state and local taxes. Thus, naturally most state and local governments were strongly opposed to the levy.

The Ways and Means Committee in measured terms advocated putting the tax on. They admitted to having some constitutional doubts but said quite pointedly that "justice requires that at least in time of war the holders of such securities should share the burdens equally with the holders of Liberty Bonds."[37]

In writing the provision the committee had ignored a suggestion of McAdoo and several Treasury experts to maintain the exemption but spread it over the brackets of each taxpayer.[38] A taxpayer in consequence would figure his income without the exemption and apply the proper rates. Then, if, say 20 percent of his income came from tax exempt securities, he could take 20 percent off his taxes. Treasury legal experts said this would get around the constitutional problems while mitigating the use of the bonds to avoid taxes.

The provision as written unleashed a torrid debate on the House floor, but all attempts at amendment were beaten back.[39] The Senate Finance Committee's hearings were deluged with witnesses and petitions from state and local governments urging that the section be removed. In response, the provision was taken out, with the report simply wryly noting that it was unfair to tax these bonds if the states could not tax federal obligations. On the Senate floor progressives tried to have the tax reinstated but failed. In the conference committee the House receded and the holders of state and local bonds remained beyond the Treasury's reach.

The salaries of state and local officials occasioned a similar legal debate. Ways and Means also provided for their assessment, again successfully fending off House floor challenges. The Finance Committee left this provision in the bill, only to have it taken out on the floor. In the conference committee the House again receded.

Judges and presidents did not fare so well. Ways and Means

included their salaries within the law's purview also. The Finance Committee agreed and the Senate did not remove this item on the floor. There was little reason, therefore, for conference to tamper with it.

Two items affecting deductions were inserted in this law, both by Ways and Means. First, the $200 exemption for a dependent child under eighteen was extended "to cover persons receiving their chief support from the taxpayer who are incapable of self-support because mentally or physically defective."[40] The second was allowing full deductibility of losses incurred in nonregular business transactions. It will be remembered that the 1917 law allowed those losses only to the extent of similar gains. Several persons testified at the Ways and Means hearings concerning this, and Kitchin indicated he had thought a good deal about it himself. It was put in at this stage and received remarkably little discussion throughout, emerging unscathed in the final bill.

The rising rates led to the bringing of the problem of single-year accounting to Congress's attention. Many types of businesses do not have a year as their normal operating cycle. Further, some businesses, such as farming, are subject to wild swings in income. One could easily lose $5000 a year for two years and incur large debts. Then, if one made $10,000 the third year, the loans could be repaid. Nevertheless, a tax would be owed on the entire $10,000. After hearing from several witnesses and listening to Senator Jones's description of how a similar provision worked in Britain, the Finance Committee admitted that "under our present high rates of taxation, [this] may often result in grave injustice."[41] The solution was to adopt a one-year loss carryback and carryforward.

On the floor Senator Lenroot (a former member of Ways and Means and winner of the special April Senatorial election in Wisconsin) launched an attack against this idea.[42] It was something entirely new in American tax laws, he said, and in effect created periods of two or three years for income measurement. In a depression, moreover, profitable businesses would have to bear an even greater share of the burden since the lost revenue would have to be made up somewhere. Jones, in reply, admitted that it was not an ideal solution, but that it is an inherently difficult problem. Since the British have more experience with income taxation than we, and their setup seems to be working reasonably well, he argued, this is just as good an approach overall as any. As for revenue, not all businesses, he contended, are going to be losing money at the same time. Thus, there will be an aggregate balancing. Lenroot was still not satisfied but the committee version was adopted (35–17).

Once again the question of how to handle holding companies came up. The 1917 provisions were not working any better than had the 1916 ones, but the Treasury staff had no new ideas. Kitchin came up with the notion of allowing corporations to deduct dividends from their normal tax. This would therefore get the money into the hands of individuals where it could be taxed at higher rates. The Finance Committee deleted this provision, perhaps seeing its fallacy, and went back to the pre-1917 strategy. If a corporation were formed for the purpose of avoiding the tax, it would be taxed as a partnership (meaning each stockholder must report all the income to which he is entitled in the year it is earned). In the conference committee the Senators prevailed again.

For businesses engaged in the sale or manufacture of any type of product, calculating an inventory is essential to determining income.[43] After a physical count is taken, a cost must be assigned. If all the goods on hand at the beginning of the year plus those purchased during the year cost the same, there is no problem. But what if a merchant has on hand January 1 10 widgets which cost $10 each. During the year he purchases 20 more, 10 at $11 each and 10 at $12 each. At the end of the year he has eight left. What is the inventory value? Or, what if by December 31 the widget market has fallen to $5?

Accounting theory had not yet accepted the last in, first out method for stock in trade. This meant that inventories were taken at first in, first out. The effect of this in a period of rising prices is to inflate earnings, or in the more popular phrase, create "paper profits."[44] Arguing that this had happened, business interests flocked to Washington to argue that they should, if prices fell dramatically, be able to take a loss for inventory shrinkage. In reality, this is a boon because the losses will be recognized in the following period's income statement anyway (if inventory pricing procedures are followed consistently). Further, the new loss carryback and carryforward would cure much of the problem in any event. Nevertheless, both committees wrote this provision into the law (restricting it to 1919). The commissioner was given the power, though, to determine whether such losses had actually occurred.

The final major issue was the mine and oil and gas well depletion issue. Both committees spent several days listening to testimony and complained of being "lobbied heavily."[45] Adding to the controversy was the question of what any particular proposal might do to the current production of oil, coal, and iron, items which were critical to the war effort.

The oil men complained primarily of two items in the tax law. One was the limitation of depletion to the cost of the producing well. The other was the way gains were calculated on sales. The basis of a piece of property, in this case a lease, was merely the cost of that individual piece of property.

"Wildcatters," or small-time operators who look for oil, begin by leasing land. Next, they drill for oil, turning up mostly "dry holes." Wildcatters usually spend several years and a lot of money in the search for oil, hoping to hit that one well that will make their quest worthwhile. For tax purposes, however, the depletion allowance, to allow a return of capital before income taxation began, was limited to the cost of the one producing well. Would it not be more equitable to allow the wildcatter the costs sunk into dry holes as part of his capital?

Any deduction for depletion taken by a wildcatter would assume that he developed and pumped the well. In practice, though, these men usually sell their lease to someone such as Standard Oil. Of course the sales price reflects the capitalized value of the oil that everyone now knows is there. Let us say a wildcatter has drilled nine dry holes at a cost of $10,000 each. On the tenth, also costing $10,000, he strikes oil. If he now sells the lease to Standard Oil for $300,000, what is the taxable gain? Under the 1917 law it was $290,000. The contention of the oil people was that a gain of $200,000 ($300,000—10 × $10,000) was the actual figure. (The 1916 depletion allowance was quite adequate for the new owner since their cost was the new market value of the property. Consequently, it was not the big oil companies that appeared before the committees but the smaller independent producers and their attorneys.)

The Ways and Means Committee listened to pleas that the depletion allowance be set at 20 percent of the amount taken out each year without a limitation. Kitchin said that was much too generous and got it lowered to 10 percent. The oil people apparently thought the real test would come in the Senate, though, and bided their time.

Several of their number came to the Finance hearings to lay before the committee detailed accounts of wells, their costs, their percentage flows, the value of oil to national defense, the character of wildcatters, and the problems the tax law was causing with sales. One said no sales of leases had occurred at all within the last year in his section of Oklahoma.

Of far more credibility, though, were M. L. Requa, director of the Oil Division of the Fuel Administration and the division's attorney, Norman Beecher. Beecher said the best way around the problem was to ditch the House version since it said nothing about sales. To be equitable, the law could either allow depletion on all expenses a wildcatter had incurred in looking for oil or base it on the value of the well when a strike is made. *In the aggregate*, he said, most wildcatters spend about the market value of a well in prospecting for it. The market price has the further advantage of being easily ascertainable. "A man brings in a well producing a certain number of barrels in a certain field, and that commands a market price more stable than the price of stocks."[46]

Beecher was asked by the committee to draw up an amendment incorporating these ideas. He did so, having it allow depletion to be based on the market value of the well at the time of discovery or December 31 of any subsequent year, the date to be chosen only once by the taxpayer. Next, the surtax payable on any bona fide sale of an oil well was to be limited to 20 percent of the sales price. Although all admitted the valuation date for depletion was uncertain, these amendments were endorsed by the oil industry.[47] The Finance Committee changed the valuation date to any time within a twelve-month period after discovery, and the Senate limited that to thirty days.

Mine owners now pressed for adoption of a similar 20 percent limitation, which was granted. They also asked for the right to capitalize mine improvements, which was also granted. This latter provision meant that instead of having to take the deduction when the improvements were made, perhaps in a year of low income, owners could spread the deduction over several years. An offset would then be available for high income years. The timber industry followed with a demand for the same allowance for sawmills. This request was also granted.[48]

The Revenue Act of 1918 was a turning point in the income tax's development in several ways. It marked the last of the great wartime revenue bills, bills which had seen the income tax produce more revenue than once thought possible for any tax. Never again was its value to the national treasury to be doubted. The bill was also the final attempt at bipartisanship, with the loosening of those bonds evident especially by the war's end. The strains of partisan politics were protruding everywhere, but on the floor the minority leaders continued to repeat the now familiar plea that the bill was not perfect but nevertheless deserving of support.

It is difficult to say with any certainty what effects the practice of full committee participation had on the law's development. However, the political complexion of the Democratic center of gravity on Ways and Means and Finance was pronouncedly different from that of the full committee. Given the intricacies of group decision making, it stands to reason that the effects were surely there.

Interestingly, there was absolutely no talk of repeal in 1918. For a policy as controversial as the income tax had been only five years before, this is little short of remarkable, especially since the tax's archenemies knew from early November that they would control Congress the following session. Perhaps it was the sheer volume of dollars the income tax put into the government's pipeline. Perhaps it was that the Republicans, by sitting with the Democrats on the tax writing committees during the war, had come to assume some responsibility for the measure. Perhaps some were biding their time hoping for a Republican presidential victory in 1920, thereby avoiding an almost certain veto of an act to repeal. Whatever the case, income taxation was now a permanent part of the revenue system.

It was the first time, this act of 1918, that the income tax was to be used essentially as a budgetary device. The idea of granting some type of exclusion to returning servicemen (in lieu of a bonus) was, of course, quite popular, and plenty of verbal patriotism accompanied its passage. However, the economic wisdom of setting up such "tax expenditures" is doubtful, as is the long run political wisdom. Measures such as this bear the designation "tax expenditure" because they employ the tax code to give someone a direct monetary benefit. The expenditure nomenclature is attached because others' taxes must be raised to cover the lost revenue. The effect, therefore, is exactly the same as if a direct payment had been made from the expenditure side of the budget. It is usually easier politically in the short run, though, to handle payouts in this fashion since it is less obvious. However, a precedent once employed is easier to resort to again. This was to be but the first of a never-ending list of proposals to effect similar tax juggling.

The debate over the rates for this bill produced what was bound to happen as the income tax moved from a mechanism for redistribution to a mechanism for raising revenue. Since in the aggregate the largest percentage of the national income is in the upper middle, middle, and lower middle groups, raising the most revenue meant increasing the normal tax. When this is done, a very high marginal bracket is created immediately above the exemption. The solution was to make the normal tax progressive by making a two (or more) tiered system. This has the effect, though, of terminating the rationale for a distinction between the normal tax and the surtax.

It is interesting that, even at war's end, there was no talk of raising the exemption. If lowering it was truly an emergency revenue measure, logic should have dictated that it now be raised along with the cutting of the normal tax. That it was not suggests either that 1) the Democrats gave this as a concession in the committee bargaining, 2) the Democrats had changed their ideology of taxation, or 3) the revenue produced by lowered exemptions made it impractical to raise them. While the evidence is not conclusive, the last rationale appears the most plausible.

As the income tax became the major revenue producer in the federal government's financial arsenal, its politics also underwent a metamorphosis. During its first few years of life, it was little more than a nuisance to the well-off. By 1918, however, it was much more progressive and applied to many more citizens. It extracted sizeable sums from a large number of people and did so in an obvious way.

We have already alluded to how the question of rates was side-stepped by affected interests. More than likely this was from a due prudence exercised during wartime. What they could press for, however, was special treatment of some items of receipt or expenditure. Lowering income by either of these expedients could mean substantial savings on one's tax bill. Hence, Congress was to be faced from this point on with pressure from various economic interests to alter this or that section of the tax code. Of course, once such an exception was granted, others presented themselves pressing analogous arguments, frequently with some justice.

The oil depletion issue illustrates that at this session. There is something plausible about allowing a wildcatter to include his dry well expenses in his depletion allowance. One could make an argument, although this is far less certain, that for administrative convenience the market price of the property after discovery could be a ballpark estimate of his expenditures.[49] But if that position be granted to oil interests, why not to other types of extractive industries? If, as a further example, coal mining companies can capitalize mine improvements, a reasonable provision, why should not timber cutters capitalize sawmill improvements? And so on ad infinitum.

The result is not only a panoply of interest groups pleading that their business is different and deserving of some special treatment; it is also that the code itself becomes more complex. This very complexity creates its own anomalies, which means more attempts must be made at rectification. This in turn begets more complexity, leading to an unbreakable cycle.

It is not only the calculation of business income which is witness to this process. The extension of the $200 exemption is another good example. There is certainly an argument to be made supporting a broadening of the exemption to include those over eighteen who are dependent on the taxpayer. A mentally retarded sibling or an invalid grandparent is as much a drain on the taxpayer's resources as a child. The trouble is that there is no end to these arguments.

Cordell Hull perhaps summed it up best.

A possible danger to the successful and permanent operation of an income-tax law, as is true of all tax laws, is the disposition of its friends to insert additional exemptions here and there and to add liberal qualifications, thereby opening many doors to those who would evade or avoid their full share of taxes.[50]

NOTES

1. Letter from McAdoo to Kitchin, June 5, 1918. Reprinted in U.S. Congress, House, Committee on Ways and Means, *Hearings on the Proposed Revenue Act of 1918*, 65th Cong., 2nd sess., Part I, 9–12.

2. *Ibid.*

3. *New York Times*, May 10, 1918.

4. Seward W. Livermore, *Politics is Adjourned: Wilson and the War Congress* (Middleton, Conn.: Wesleyan University Press, 1966), 115–22.

5. Mary Synon, *McAdoo: The Man and His Times* (Indianapolis: Bobbs-Merrill, 1924), 231.

6. Cordell Hull, *The Memoirs of Cordell Hull* (New York: Macmillan, 1948), Vol. I, 95–96.

7. *New York Times*, May 21, 1918.

8. Synon, *McAdoo*, 232; *New York Times*, May 22, 1918.

9. *New York Times*, May 24, 1918.

10. *New York Times*, May 26, 1918.

11. The text is reprinted in Ways and Means Committee, *Hearings*, I, 5–8.

12. U.S. Congress, *Congressional Record*, 65th Cong., 2nd sess., May 28, 1918.

13. Synon, *McAdoo*, 228–44.

14. Kitchin's health problems and how they affected his political activity are discussed in Larry Ingle, "The Dangers of Reaction: Repeal of the Revenue Act of 1918," *North Carolina Historical Review*, XLIV (Winter, 1967), 72–88.

15. Synon, *McAdoo*, Chap. 6.

16. *New York Times*, May 29, 1918.

17. *New York Times*, June 1, 1918.

18. Ways and Means Committee, *Hearings*, I, 14.

19. *Ibid.*, 15.

20. Because of this the Fourth Liberty Loan was to bear tax-free interest.

21. U.S. Congress, Senate, Committee on Finance, *Report to Accompany H.R. 12863*, 65th Cong., 2nd sess., Senate Report No. 617, 2.

22. See Livermore, *Politics is Adjourned*, 135ff.

23. *Ibid.*, 125–34.

24. See Simmons' statement on the floor for December 10, 1918. The Senate debate on December 21 also dealt with this issue.

25. See the minority report filed by the Republicans appended to Finance Committee, *Report to Accompany H.R. 12863*.

26. *New York Times*, September 30, 1918.

27. See the testimony of Dr. Thomas Adams of the Treasury Department during the Ways and Means hearings.

28. Synon, *McAdoo*, 239.

29. *New York Times*, August 17, 1918.

30. *New York Times*, August 21, 1918.

31. *New York Times*, August 27, 1918.

32. U.S. Congress, House, Committee on Ways and Means, *Report to Accompany H.R. 12863*, 65th Cong., 1st sess., House Report No. 767, 4–5.

33. Finance Committee, *Report*, 4.

34. *Congressional Record*, December 19, 1918.

35. Ways and Means Committee, *Report*, 3.

36. *Congressional Record*, September 23, 1918; October 10, 1918; and December 23, 1918.

37. Ways and Means Committee, *Report*, 9.

38. *New York Times*, August 29, 1918.

39. *Congressional Record*, September 16, 1918.

40. Ways and Means Committee, *Report*, 5.

41. Finance Committee, *Report*, 8.

42. *Congressional Record*, December 16, 1918.

43. Net income is calculated as follows:

Sales		XXXX
Cost of goods sold:		
Beginning inventory	XXXX	
Purchases	+XXXX	
Cost of goods available for sale	XXXX	
Ending inventory	−XXXX	
Cost of goods sold	XXXX	−XXXX
Gross profit		XXXX
Expenses		−XXXX
Net income		XXXX

44. To illustrate:

Sales (S) = 100,000
Expenses (E) = 25,000
Beginning inventory (BI) 30,000
Purchases during the year (P) = 90,000
Ending inventory (EI) Case 1 = 50,000; Case 2 = 65,000
Calculating Net income (NI) and Cost of goods sold (CGS):

$$NI = S - CGS - E$$
$$CGS = BI + P - EI$$

Case 1: $CGS = 30,000 + 90,000 - 50,000$
$\qquad\qquad = 70,000$
$\qquad NI = 100,000 - 70,000 - 25,000$
$\qquad\qquad = 5,000$
Case 2: $CGS = 30,000 + 90,000 - 65,000$
$\qquad\qquad = 55,000$
$\qquad NI = 100,000 - 55,000 - 25,000$
$\qquad\qquad = 20,000$

45. *Congressional Record*, February 8, 1919.

46. U.S. Congress, Senate, Committee on Finance, *Hearings on H.R. 12863*, 65th Cong., 2nd sess., Part III, 46.

47. Finance Committee, *Hearings*, III, October 18, 1918.

48. *Ibid.*, *passim*.

49. The effect of this was also to make wildcatting even more of a speculative enterprise than before. If one hit a well early, the returns could be enormous. Not a few fortunes were made by such lucky prospectors. (Of course, any number were also lost.)

50. *Congressional Record*, September 10, 1918.

IV

The Revenue Act of 1921

THE END OF WORLD WAR I brought both a changed political and economic climate to the United States.[1] Necessary peacetime economic conversions were accompanied by the anguished debate over League membership. As for the federal budget, expenditures were falling as military contracts were completed and the wartime bureaucratic apparatus dismantled.

The election of 1920 was fought over issues other than taxation. In it, though, both parties indicated support for general tax reduction as well as the elimination of many war levies, without either being any more specific. Soon after the Republican victory, a rewriting of the nation's revenue laws was scheduled.

President Harding was neither a dynamic leader nor an expert on tax matters. He much preferred the role of arbitrator and mediator, leaving the initiative in the hands of others. Moreover, while he shared his party's favorable outlook toward business, he was not wedded to any particular substantive tax policies. He once confided to a friend, "I can't make a damn thing out of this tax problem. I listen to one side and they seem right, and then—God!—I talk to the other side and they seem just as right."[2]

In financial matters, Harding leaned heavily on Andrew Mellon, his secretary of the treasury. In meetings, Mellon seldom spoke, and never on nonfinancial matters, but when he did others in the administration tended to follow his lead. This scion of American finance had no previous political experience whatever, but did have some well-thought out ideas on taxation.[3]

It was risk capital, he believed, that was the engine of economic growth. Without continuing investment in productive enterprises, the economy would ultimately stagnate. As a sheer matter-of-fact, it was the wealthy who provided most of society's risk capital. If, therefore, the tax system encouraged them to do other things with their money, everyone would suffer in the long run.

The 65 percent surtax rates had driven many wealthy people, he argued, to put their money into tax exempt state and local bonds. By and large, the data tend to support him. In 1918, from those with incomes over $50,000 the government collected $917,000,000 in income taxes. By 1919 this had fallen to $587,000,000 and by 1920 to $347,000,000.[4] This was in spite of the fact that the war had swollen the ranks of those in this bracket. Mellon viewed this with alarm and believed a sharp reduction was needed in these maximum surtax rates. In fairness, he also proposed, though with less enthusiasm, ending the exempt status of these securities.[5]

The chairmanships of the revenue committees were now in the hands of Joseph Fordney and Boies Penrose.[6] Fordney, on Ways and Means, was a self-made Michigan lumberman with only three months of formal schooling. He entered politics late in life, at the urging of local Republican leaders looking for a "clean" candidate after a small scandal had been exposed. He had few ideas, read little, and led a simple life. He was a strong believer in protective tariffs, though, and a foe of high taxation generally. Although not a good speaker, he could exercise strong leadership in small groups. Originally elected in 1898, he was serving his last term in Congress.

Penrose was Fordney's opposite in background. From a prominent Philadelphia family, he attended all the best schools. After Harvard, he read law, practiced with an eminent Philadelphia firm, and became involved in Republican politics. Working his way up quickly through the ranks, before long he became the kingpin of the Pennsylvania Republican machine. Like Fordney, he was not an effective speaker but was known as a master of backroom intrigue. Throughout his career, he had stood consistently against progressive policies generally. Once a robust man, he was now dying of cancer. Deprived of his energy and one-half of his weight, this was to be his swan song. On the last day of 1921 he died quietly. One suspects that his illness was largely responsible for his inability to exercise as much leadership on the Republican side as usual.

The man in line to become chairman of the Finance Committee was Porter McCumber of North Dakota. He was known as more knowledgeable on tax issues than the other two. Undoubtedly, though, he had to be cautious throughout 1921 so as not to appear to be undercutting an ailing party oligarch. Too, he was in political trouble in North Dakota, evidenced by the fact that he was to lose his party's primary in 1922.

Worthy of at least mention was the situation on the Democratic side in the House. Kitchin had suffered a stroke and was confined to his bed in Scotland Neck, North Carolina. From there, he still tried to maintain control of the caucus and direct the fight against the revenue bill. John Nance Garner (Texas) had assumed on-the-spot leadership on Ways and Means, but he had all the problems of an heir apparent while the king still lives. Furthermore, the Democrats were in the usual state of disarray that strikes a party after a crushing defeat at the polls.

The political complications were different from those of the war years. To begin with, there was not now the need for bipartisanship. Yet, the pattern of legislative activity during the war had created its own institutional inertia. While no one expected the full meetings of the tax committees to continue making substantive decisions, the return to majority party domination was interrupted, especially in the Senate, by jolts of one sort or another. Sometimes a dissident might threaten to side with the Democrats in committee as well as take a dispute to the full caucus. When coupled with Penrose's diminished effectiveness and a lack of leadership from the White House, this made the Senate decision-making process very fluid.

The termination of the war and the depression which soon set in also wrought havoc to the budget projections. In addition, the Washington Naval Conference was in session at this time, giving many people reason to hope that further reductions were in the offing. On top of these uncertainties, Congress passed the Budget and Accounting Act of 1921 during this period. As its implementation began, under the dynamic General Dawes, it introduced new confusion.

Even at this point, there was spirited debate about the war debts. If they were paid as scheduled they could be used to reduce the national debt, reduce taxes, or for some designated expenditure object. The question was whether tax planning should even take them into account.

Congress was also considering two new expenditure programs of large magnitude. One was the universally popular highway construction program. Federal aid to states to assist in road building went back to 1913, but now it was proposed to erect a massive interstate highway system with one-half federal participation.[7] The other, much more politically volatile, was the idea of a soldier's bonus. The American Legion and ex-servicemen generally were campaigning vigorously for some such bonus to be paid to all veterans. The enormous cost led Mellon to demur, and he quickly won over the president. Few Republican politicians shared their misgivings, but could not budge either. (Later, Harding was to veto a bonus bill.) Its effect at this congressional session was to unleash a horde of attempts to amend the revenue bill seeking to pledge part of it to a bonus.

Senator Reed Smoot of Utah, with backing from various business interests, hatched the idea of a national sales tax. He offered it in various forms—a manufacturer's tax, a wholesale tax, and a retail tax—and with varying rates. It could be used in place of all excise taxes, he said, and make up the lost revenue from lowering income tax rates. In spite of business backing, however, he was unable to secure approval in several tries on the Senate floor. As a final ploy, he tried linking it to the bonus, but that too failed.

Politically, the most important development was within the Republican party. Although the GOP had swept to power in 1920, it was hardly unified. Of several fissures, the most important was the one that pitted Senators and Representatives from western and agricultural states against those from the East. Variously called the "agricultural bloc" or the "western bloc" (which were somewhat different), the former would often threaten to make common cause with the Democrats on certain issues. High on this list, as in 1909, was taxation. While Robert LaFollette had gone too far to be an effective leader, men such as William Borah of Idaho and Albert Cummins of Iowa commanded a following.[8] The president's desire to maintain party harmony led him to continually seek conciliation with the bloc; also, he was often made painfully aware of the fact that massive Republican desertions over taxes might well jeopardize other administration measures. Harding's willingness to deal with them, though, only served to strengthen their hand.

Soon after his inauguration, Harding huddled with congressional leaders to discuss the major problems he was facing.[9] Tariff revision, favored by farmers, and tax reduction, pressed by business, were given highest priority. Fordney and Penrose both urged calling a special session but offered conflicting views on which of these should come first. Fordney was for an emergency tariff; Penrose for tax reform. On March 14 Harding issued the call for the special session but could not settle on priorities. Instead, he chose to play for time, giving each group the impression he agreed with them. The following week Fordney and Penrose worked out a compromise whereby Ways and Means would take up the tariff and the Finance Committee would begin hearings on tax legislation.

Harding opened the special session with what is usually accorded to be the best speech of his presidency, enunciating some far-reaching ideas on a range of topics. On taxes he had this to say:

> I know of no more pressing problem at home than to restrict our national expenditures within the limits of our national income, and at the same time measurably lift the burdens of war taxation from the shoulders of the American people.
>
> A prompt and thoroughgoing revision of the internal tax laws, made with due regard to the protection of the revenue, is in my judgment, a requisite to the revival of business activity in this country.[10]

In late May the Ways and Means Committee, having disposed of the tariff question, asked Mellon for his tax recommendations. It held some perfunctory hearings in July and quickly reported a bill along the lines Mellon suggested. Although Democratic opposition was to be expected, western and farm state Republicans also signaled defection from their party's proposals. In a key meeting of the Republican caucus the farm bloc, by a 96–87 vote, forced Fordney to agree to a year's delay in implementation.[11] It was a small victory, but it contained important portents.

With this compromise, Fordney brought the bill to the House floor August 16. Securing a special motion, he managed to have the bill voted on merely four days later. Passage was assured, 274–125.

Meanwhile, the Senate had become hopelessly mired down on

several issues. By mid-July it was debating the Bonus Bill, the only question which could secure enough consensus to even be brought to the floor, when the president decided to intervene. In a dramatic personal appearance before the Senate, Harding urged immediate action on the tax bill and a shelving of the bonus.[12]

The president's action did lead to the dropping of the bonus proposal for the time being but left many Senators irate for various reasons—opposition to the tax bill, a desire for the bonus, a distaste for executive "meddling" in Senate affairs. Adding this to the split in the Republican party and Penrose's ineffective leadership constituted a recipe for political fallout. Coalitions formed and reformed on various amendments to the tax proposal. Surtax rates especially were forced up, but debate dragged on over a multitude of other proposals. Finally, after fifteen continuous hours of consideration, a vote was taken November 7. Passage was by a 38–24 margin.

However, the Senate had almost rewritten the bill, adding 833 amendments.[13] The conferees, of course, would have preferred few, if any, of the important ones; nevertheless, they knew they stood no chance of carrying the upper chamber if they sabotaged all of them. Then, buoyed by the bloc's success in the Senate, a movement began in the House to instruct its conferees to accept the Senate rates. Harding sought to intervene again and effect a compromise. But the bloc instead united with the Democrats and secured the instructions in a 201–173 vote. (Ninety-four Republicans deserted the president.)

Except for the usual shouting and recriminations, it was now all over. The conferees took out a few of the most distasteful amendments, gambling on acceptance of the package. The House quickly approved the compromise and the Senate finally did so, but only 39–29 and after a rancorous debate. Harding signed it November 23, fifteen minutes after it passed the Senate.

By far the most important controversy at this revision was over the surtax rates. The economy's need for and the political appeal of tax reduction were obvious to all. It was a question of whose taxes to lower and by how much. Other taxes than the income levy were popular targets for reduction or elimination, especially the cumbersome excess profits tax. But it was the income tax that had assumed center stage. It not only struck more people than ever before, but its revenue-producing capabilities made the whole government budget extremely sensitive to any alterations.

Certainly, no one was surprised that the Republicans proposed lowering taxes mainly on the well-to-do. It was rather the extent of their reductions compared to those of middle and lower income persons that caused the political firestorm. In fact, the last two Democratic treasury secretaries had proposed dropping surtax rates at the top levels. Carter Glass had said in his 1919 report:

> The upmost brackets of the surtax have already passed the point of productivity and . . . drive possessors of these great incomes more and more to place their wealth in the billions of dollars of wholly exempt securities . . . issued by States and municipalities.[14]

David Houston had added in 1920:

> It seems idle to speculate in the abstract as to whether or not a progressive income tax schedule rising to rates in excess of 70% is justifiable. We are confronted with a condition, not a theory. The fact is that such rates can not be successfully collected. . . . For the year 1916 net income amounting to $992,972,885 was included in the returns of taxpayers having net income over $300,000 per year.
>
> This aggregate fell to $731,372,153 for the year 1917 and to $392,247,329 for the year 1918. There is little reason to believe that the actual income of the richer tax-payers of the country had fallen in the interval. It is the taxable income which has been reduced and almost certainly through investment by the richer taxpayers in tax-exempt properties.[15]

Mellon reiterated the same message in his testimony before the Ways and Means Committee. He argued that a maximum 40 percent total tax was satisfactory, but that 20 percent would produce "at least as much revenue." The Ways and Means bill brought the top surtaxes down to 32 percent (which would give a 40 percent total when combined with the 8 percent normal tax) and made it effective at $66,000. Otherwise, it kept the normal tax as it was and the surtax on incomes below $66,000 largely intact. Whatever the economic wisdom of this proposal, its political effect was to forge a coalition of Democrats and Republican dissidents. While the party faithful held in the House, but only, remember, after the move to defer implementation, Senate Republican opposition could not be contained.

When the Republicans on Finance got down to serious business, they voted 5–4 to scale the surtaxes up from 32 percent at $66,000 to 50 percent on incomes over $200,000. Significantly, Penrose cast the deciding vote.[16] By the time the bill was brought up on the Senate floor, the political situation had gone from fluid to chaotic. Every rate proposal had more opponents than backers. Finally, the 50 percent compromise seemed the only possible hope, and an exasperated Senate approved it 54–13.

In the House meantime, the bloc had been serving notice that it would cause Fordney trouble. Harding tried several times to work out a compromise, but to no avail. Democrats and House bloc leaders moved to tie Fordney's hands at the conference by offering a motion to instruct House conferees to accept the Senate rates. Harding and his allies decided on a Presidential letter strategy, suggesting a 40 percent compromise.[17] Unfortunately, the bloc would have none of it, and the motion to instruct passed handily. With the House conferees bound and ineffective Senate leaders looking over their shoulders, the 50 percent compromise became law.

Even though the normal tax was not formally modified, it was in effect lowered by other provisions. For a head of family with less than $5,000 income, the Ways and Means Committee thought $500 should be added to the exemption he now enjoyed. At the end, this provision was still in the bill. Ways and Means also sought to raise the exemption for dependents from $200 to $400, a proposal which also emerged unscathed. On the Senate floor there was a brief attempt to raise the age of allowable dependency from eighteen to twenty-one. It would allow, the argument went, parents to continue to claim the exemption when they were the principal means of support, as when the child is a college student. It was rejected, however.

The question of stock dividends had been settled once and for all by a court case, *Eisner v. Macomber*, 257 U.S. 189. The Treasury had lost the case and the opinion left Congress little choice but to omit future stock dividends from income, which was done without dispute.

Taxation of capital gains was finally recognized in this act. It was widely alleged that full taxation of such transactions was holding up normal business adjustments, a contention that probably had some basis in fact. The Ways and Means Committee recommended that the tax be limited to 15 percent on such transactions, while the Finance Committee opted for 16 percent. On the Senate floor there was an extended debate over this provision. First, there was disagreement over exactly what constituted a capital gain. One recommendation would have included all property held more than one year while another pressed for three. Two years naturally emerged as the easy compromise. Senator Lenroot tried to have stocks and bonds exempted from the special levy, something he succeeded in having the Senate agree to, only to watch it taken out at the conference.

The problem with setting a capital gains rate is that the higher it is, the higher the income level one must be in to take advantage of it. If, for example, the rate is set at 15 percent, anyone with a marginal rate of less than 15 percent will opt to pay his regular tax. Ironically, therefore, those favoring more progressive taxation must push to lower the capital gains rate if such a provision is set up in the law. Only by so doing can those in lower brackets benefit from it. After much discussion in the Senate, 12 percent was adopted. One idea which did not win acceptance was to include only 40 percent of the capital gain in income. This would have spread the tax break throughout the brackets. It was rejected without a roll call, however. An amendment was added, nevertheless, that the total tax of those claiming capital gains had to be at least 12 percent of income. This prohibited capital gains taxation from being coupled with other tax avoidance devices to reduce taxes below a minimum.

As the tax rates had risen, taxpayers sought out and stumbled on ever more devices to structure their affairs in such a way as to avoid the bite. Several states had and have what are known as community property laws.[18] Although varying to some degree, they all provide that any property acquired during a marriage belongs one-half to each spouse. What residents of these states began doing therefore was filing two tax returns, one for the husband and one for the wife, assigning one-half their total income to each. By so doing they were getting double mileage out of the exemption as well as making their income fall into lower brackets than it would if lumped together. Naturally, the greater the income, the higher the marginal bracket and the greater the saving.

The Treasury had suggested that for the sake of equity all income of persons in those states should be assigned to "the spouse having the management and control of the community property."[19] In all eight the husband was given this role. In practical terms, therefore, one spouse (usually the wife) could file only for the income over which she had management; the husband's earnings could not then be split. Ways and Means wrote this into the bill, and Finance kept it. However, on the Senate floor those from community property states made endless speeches about the value of diversity in a federal system and the degree to which their states cared about women. Apparently, the tax fate of their upper income constituents was of no concern to them. In any event, they must have convinced their colleagues, who probably needed their votes on other measures, of the justness of their cause. In conference the House receded. It was to be another day, therefore, before Congress would take the easy way out and extend the benefits of community property to everyone through the mechanism of the joint return.

The receipt of income in kind was also the subject of an amendment. Many members of the clergy traditionally receive the use of a house as part of their compensation. On theoretical grounds, the rental value should be included in income. As a practical matter, however, it creates no cash with which to pay the tax. Moreover, clergy normally have low salaries to start with. However, their social status meant that no one would mount a serious political attack on them. On the Senate floor, Senator Dial of South Carolina offered an amendment to exempt the rental value of parsonages when furnished as part of a minister's compensation. No objection was raised, not even by the Finance Committee.

The net loss carryover and carryback provision, enacted in 1918 as a temporary measure to allow for wartime readjustments, was made permanent for carryforwards. Ways and Means included the permanent extension in its recommendations, and no one seemed to object. In design and purpose, this is a reasonable provision. However, there is no agreed upon standard as to how long losses should be able to be carried forward. Here, the one-year rule of 1918 was doubled without much discussion. Before long, though, business interests were pushing for longer periods, which have since been granted. Too, a logical corollary of the permanent loss carryforward is the permanent loss carryback. Ultimately, this too would become law. However reasonable and just these modifications appear, they do lower tax receipts from those taking advantage of them, and the difference must be made up somewhere.

Ingenious ways of avoiding the tax laws while remaining within the letter of the law were quickly becoming part of upper class American folklore. Two such devices used to accomplish this end were wash sales and gifts before sales. The former occurred when the value of securities had fallen to a lower price on December 31 than when an investor bought them. What he would do is sell the stock on December 31 and buy it back on January 1 or soon thereafter. He could then claim a loss on his tax return but still have the stock. Of course there was a minor element of risk, but the odds were with the investor. Concerning the latter, the law provided that property acquired by gift had as its basis its fair market value at the time of receipt. If one had paid, say, $10,000 for a piece of property ten years ago but it was now worth $50,000, a sale would produce a taxable gain of $40,000. If a man gave the property to his wife, though, immediately before the sale and she sold it, there would be no gain at all.

Congress, to its credit, moved to demolish these gimmicks. First, it disallowed any losses on securities if the same securities were repurchased within thirty days. As for gifts, the law was changed to make their basis the same as it had in the hands of the giver. Plus, it should be remembered that the capital gains tax would remove some of the incentive for this anyway.

Another significant addition to the law was the broadening of the types of organizations which could receive tax deductible contributions. The Cleveland Foundation appeared before the Senate Finance Committee to urge that gifts to foundations be made deductible.[20] The New York Community Trust requested the same treatment for donations to community chests. Senator Lodge also wanted American Legion posts included. During Ways and Means's hearings various people argued for broadening the definition to include groups organized "for a public purpose."[21] Examples cited were the National Child Labor Committee and the American Association for Labor Legislation. (Both these were primarily lobbying organizations.) The Indiana Association of CPA's even recommended chambers of commerce and civic bodies (subject to some limitations) as candidates for inclusion. The final provision allowed a deduction for gifts to:

> The United States, any State, Territory, or any political subdivision thereof, or the District of Columbia, for exclusively public purposes [or] any corporation, or community chest, fund, or foundation, organized and operated exclusively for religious, charitable, scientific, literary, or educational purposes, including posts of the American Legion or the women's auxiliary units thereof, or for the prevention of cruelty to children or animals.

The contrast with the 1918 law can best be seen by direct comparison. By its terms the eligibles were:

> Corporations organized and operated exclusively for religious, charitable, scientific, or educational purposes, or for the prevention of cruelty to children or animals.

In addition to the movements to broaden the coverage of this provision, many wished to raise the limit from 15 percent of income to 25 percent. Despite a good bit of discussion, the lower figure was kept.

A few other, relatively minor, changes were also made. One was to allow for full deductibility of outside losses. It will be recalled that this had been discussed at length earlier. This time it was adopted with only a modicum of debate. The other item was the exemption of gains from "involuntary conversions." If a persons's house burns, for example, the insurance company pays him fair market value, and he rebuilds a similar house. He now has property worth more than he did originally. To be theoretically consistent, there is a taxable gain. However, the person did not seek the gain, in many cases would rather have been without it, and has no money income. If taxed, he might have to sell the house to pay the tax. The law provided, therefore, that if there were prompt reinvestment of the settlement proceeds in similar property, there would be no taxable gain.

Pensions paid to veterans were decreed to be nontaxable. Although the Democratic leadership entered a dissent on the grounds that it should be on a sliding scale, the veteran's advocates prevailed this time.

There was one other major amendment adopted in the Senate which failed to make it through the hostile conference committee. Robert LaFollette obtained passage of his idea to make all returns open to the public and to require that all persons submit a list of their tax-exempt securities along with their returns. This was strongly assailed by the Old Guard in both the Senate and the House, and Fordney and Penrose got it taken out in conference. LaFollette was then unable to get Senate rejection of the whole report. Apparently, many people feared this provision more than some of the other Democratic-bloc amendments.

One issue which got only a nod, but which would become more and more important, was the method of figuring depreciation. As noted before, the law allowed a reasonable deduction for "exhaustion, wear and tear." The Treasury had issued some regulations, but many felt Congress should be more specific.[22] Since this item is critical in the calculation of business income, it would continue to need attention.

In many ways the Revenue Act of 1921 was more of a turning point for the income tax than that of 1918. Or, perhaps it should be said that it reached another plateau in its development and its place became assured in the financial picture. For both the executive and the legislature were now firmly in the hands of those bitterly opposed to the whole idea only eight years earlier. There was not, however, one serious utterance about repeal.

A couple of people testifying at the congressional hearings did advocate repeal, but no one paid any attention. Senator Smoot's sales tax was no doubt aimed indirectly at the income tax, but not even he dared say so publicly. In the initial hearings before Ways and Means, Dr. Thomas Adams, a Treasury expert employed by the Democrats but retained by the Republicans, had this to say:

This is in some senses the keynote to the whole work of tax revision. I think it is the question about which you gentlemen must make up your minds, if I may venture to say that, before you can plan the general scheme of Federal taxation for the future. Personally, I think it holds the key to the entire matter of tax revision. The question is whether there is to be or is not to be preserved a progressive income tax.[23]

Seemingly, Fordney, Penrose, and company had indeed made up their minds.

The capital gains tax is another sign of maturity in the law. At some point, capital gains had to be differentiated from ordinary income. If the practice of not taxing them at all was taboo, then some sort of special rate had to be constructed. Otherwise, the income tax would have had to suffer from continual attack on this ground. Whether or not setting the 12 percent rate is the best answer is another matter. It would appear, on several grounds, that opting for something akin to the 40 percent inclusion rule would be fairer. However, that would not have drawn a firm distinction between income and capital gains. On the other hand, the filing of capital gains returns at the same time as income tax returns (and linking them by the minimum tax provision) negated whatever virtue the move had anyway. Latter day policy makers would have to grapple with this issue time and time again.

If 1918 witnessed a change toward greater lobbying in income tax politics, 1921 saw the settling and expansion of this pattern. Small and economically weak groups showed they too could obtain favorable tax treatment, as in the case of the housing exemption for clergy. Other groups similarly situated were to learn the essentials of this game very quickly. The seeming justice, and the small individual impact on the revenue picture, of these provisions make them hard for politicians to resist. Yet it opens the door to others with similar claims, which then become even harder to resist; and while the impact of any one of these provisions is rather small, their aggregate impact is substantial.

Congress moved, also, to close two obvious loopholes. A loophole is, of course, hard to define. However, when there are blatant gaps in the law which allow for all but outright evasion, Congress has tended to shut off the practice. The trouble is that "where there is a will, there is a way." The complexity of the tax law inevitably creates situations of this type. Ironically, for example, Congress set the stage for all sorts of shenanigans at this very session by enacting the involuntary conversion section. All manner of schemes have been foisted upon the tax collector by the use of this device. This has resulted in volumes of amendments and regulations, starting the cycle all over again.[24] In short, it is a never-ending parade of plug and replug.

We also see here the tendency for a temporary concession to become permanent. Those who wanted a loss carryforward were unable to get it in 1918. Instead, they settled for a "temporary" carryforward based on war conditions. Once in, though, it was easier to extend than to kill for it then became part of the status quo. "Nothing is so permanent as a temporary tax" could have as its corollary "nothing is so permanent as a favorable temporary part of the tax law."

In addition, the parallel tendency for holes in the law to grow is clearly in evidence here. This session's broadening of organizations eligible to receive tax deductible donations signaled the growth of a giant. Every session of Congress from this point on was to bring new requests. By the 1980s it was a rare organization that did not come under the provision.

Not only was the law becoming more complex internally, it was encountering knotty problems growing out of American institutional complexity. Probably no one thought much about community property laws in 1913. However, the mess it created was and is unsolvable. Ultimately, as pointed out above, the "remedy" was the joint return. However, this created the notorious discrimination against singles. When the "rectification" of this occurred in 1969, it made the tax law contain a "marriage penalty."[25] And so it goes.

As a final note on complexity, many members of Congress loathed this very fault. One even ventured the thought that he did not think anyone in Congress could now fill out his own return. But there is no way out of complexity if one is to have a functioning tax law.[26] As another side effect, it should also be mentioned that tax advising was becoming a growth industry—something which created yet another important interest group.

The question of the rates can be viewed from several angles. On the surface, it was a conflict which pitted Mellon and Wall Street against a Democratic-Progressive Republican coalition. The former wished to cut the rates on the big boys, claiming, of course, that they were acting for the greater good of all. The latter wished, if not to soak the rich, at least to siphon a bit.

While that generalizaton is valid as a generalization, it must not be allowed to conceal other, equally valid, truths. For one thing, long before John F. Kennedy's conversion of "everyone" to Keynesianism, the tax system was being discussed as a conscious tool of fiscal policy (although, of course, that term was yet to be invented). It is likely that Mellon and his backers were only dimly aware that they were using government policy to this end, but clearly they were. They would most likely have recoiled at using the expenditure side of the budget to accomplish economic growth (as in Lyndon Johnson's Great Society programs), but they were creating a precedent.

More importantly, there is, I think, the beginnings of the use of symbolism in the rates. It is striking that all the discussions of keeping the maximum surtax rate at 50 percent rather than 32 percent had a certain unreality about them. If it were true, which seems almost beyond dispute, that the wealthy were largely escaping the high surtax rates, why keep them? Reading between the lines of speeches by bloc leaders, one gets the feeling that they were at least dimly aware of the political mileage to be gotten from keeping nominal rates quite high. This is not to say all thought this way or that it was a major motivation for any of them.

Nevertheless, if they really wanted to levy high rates, why did they not seriously go about attacking the problem? No real effort was even launched to tax state and local bond interest, although there were valid reasons to believe it was constitutional. As an alternative, they could have taken McAdoo's earlier suggestion and spread the interest throughout the brackets. Dr. Adams, in fact, proposed this to the Ways and Means Committee, but not one Congressman picked up on it. Given that either of these would have served to put more teeth into the 50 percent levy, or even a 40 percent levy, their lack of consideration gives one pause.

Lastly, we see emerging a curious phenomenon with regard to the impact of the tax law. At each revision, those at the very top and the very bottom get helped the most, with more usually going to those at the top. When the law was first enacted in 1913, there was at least an attempt to make it truly progressive throughout the income grades. By 1921 this had changed. The direct rate cuts went mostly to high income people. At the same time, the Republican-dominated Ways and Means Committee doubled the exemption for dependents and raised the head of family exemption $500 for those under $5,000. "The equity of these increased exemptions," the Committee wrote with reference to the first, "is self-evident. It relieves the taxpayers least able to bear the burden."[27] When all was said and done and Harding had signed the law, the normal tax rates were the same, the exemption level the same (with the exception noted above), and the surtaxes for those under $66,000 basically the same. The burden was clearly beginning to fall on middle income taxpayers.

NOTES

1. On the Harding presidency see Eugene P. Trani and David Wilson, *The Presidency of Warren G. Harding* (Lawrence: Regents Press of Kansas, 1977) and Robert Murray, *The Harding Era* (Minneapolis: University of Minnesota Press, 1968).

2. Murray, *Harding Era*, 185–186.

3. Andrew Mellon, *Taxation: The People's Business* (New York: MacMillan, 1924).

4. Data given in letter from Harding to Fordney, reprinted in *Congressional Record*, November 17, 1921.

5. See his testimony before the Ways and Means Committee, August 1, 1921. U.S. Congress, House, Committee on Ways and Means, *Hearings on Internal Revenue Revision*, 67th Congress, 1st session, 1921.

6. On Penrose, see Walter Davenport, *Power and Glory: The Life of Boies Penrose* (New York: Putnam, 1931) and Robert D. Bowden, *Boies Penrose: Symbol of an Era* (New York: Greenberg, 1937). For Fordney and McCumber it is necessary to consult the *Dictionary of American Biography*.

7. Treasury experts said it would add $105,000,000 to the budget. Letter from Mellon to Fordney and Penrose, November 10, 1921. Reprinted in *Congressional Record*, November 21, 1921.

8. On party politics in general see Karl Schriftgiesser, *This Was Normalcy: An Account of Party Politics During Twelve Republican Years, 1921–32* (New York: Oriole Editions, 1973; reprint of 1948 ed.) and David Bruner, *The Politics of Provincialism: The Democratic Party in Transition, 1918–32* (New York: Knopf, 1970). On the bloc's formation and its internal problems, consult Darrel Ashby, "Progressivism Against Itself: The Senate Western Bloc in the 1920's," *Mid-America*, 50 (October, 1968), 291–304.

9. Murray, *Harding Era*, 124ff; *New York Times*, March 17, 1921.

10. The speech can be found in the *New York Times* for April 13, 1921.

11. *New York Times*, August 16, 1921. The vote was, according to the *Times*, uncertain when the caucus opened. The support of James M. Mann of Illinois, a former House Republican leader, gave the bloc the victory.

12. *New York Times*, July 13, 1921.

13. A good number of these, however, were the result of the Senate changing the form of the bill.

14. U.S. Department of the Treasury, *Annual Report for 1919, 24*.

15. *U.S. Department of the Treasury, Annual Report for 1920,* 36–37.

16. *New York Times*, October 11, 1921.

17. *New York Times*, November 18, 1921. The letter is reprinted in the *Congressional Record*, November 17, 1921.

18. The states are Arizona, California, Idaho, Louisiana, New Mexico, Nevada, Texas, and Washington.

19. U.S. Congress, House, Committee on Ways and Means, *Report to Accompany H.R. 8245*, 67th Congress, 1st session, House Report No. 350,11.

20. U.S. Congress, Senate, Committee on Finance, *Hearings on the Proposed Revenue Act of 1921*, 67th Congress, 1st session.

21. Committee on Ways and Means, *Hearings*, 1921.

22. Committee on Finance, *Hearings*, 1921.

23. U.S. Congress, House, Committee on Ways and Means, *Hearings on Revenue Revision*, 67th Congress, 1st session, 1920. (These hearings were held after the election but before the inauguration.)

24. A perusal of Code Section 1033 and the associated Regulations and court decisions is recommended for the skeptical.

25. The 1969 law said that no single person would have to pay more than 20% above what a married person earning the same income would pay. If two relatively high income people contemplating marriage calculated their prospective tax burden, they would usually discover they were better off staying single and living together. In 1981, the "marriage penalty" was softened by a special deduction for two income earning couples.

26. See Kenyon E. Poole, "The Problem of Simplicity in the Enactment of Tax Legislation, 1920–40," *Journal of Political Economy*, 49 (December, 1941), 895–905.

27. Committee on Ways and Means, *Report*, 6.

V

Taxes and Politics
American Style

Surveying the foregoing narrative, two important conclusions stand out. First, the peculiarities of each Congressional session go far in explaining each outcome, an idea which contrasts sharply with those who see long-run forces at work behind the development of tax policy. Second, the complexity of income taxation leads to several different types of political processes. No single model exists which will explain the politics of all the provisions; instead, the revenue code must be disaggregated and analyzed in parts.

The Politics of Congressional Sessions

In Sidney Ratner's monumental *American Taxation*,[1] he developed a theme of policy change closely atuned to the tenets of progressive historical scholarship. The industrial revolution after the Civil War led to elite control of American national institutions. The Populists challenged this domination but failed. Progressivism, drawing much of its sustenance from Populism, fared somewhat better. While not entirely remaking America in their image, the Progressives did succeed in enacting major reform legislation. The nineteen-twenties saw an erosion of Progressivism and a return to an earlier, less savory era. Business interests were almost entirely dominant and undid much of what the Progressives had accomplished.

The depression, however, returned the reformers to power and cleared the way for another set of victories.

Tax politics in Ratner's view were largely a clash of economic elites and democratically oriented reformers. The former were largely a selfish lot who used all manner of tactics, including propagandizing various versions of the "trickle down theory," to stymie tax reform. The common man, on the other hand, continually sought to unload himself of his rather large burdens and lay a just share on the wealthy. When political conditions were ripe, the common man would rout elites from the citadels of power and take enormous strides toward securing economic justice. Excepting the valley of the age of Mellon, since 1913 the common man had emerged triumphant.

It will not demean Ratner's classic to suggest that he was wrong on several counts. This brief study of the early evolution of the income tax shows that the world is more complex than the model of progressive historiography allows.[2]

In the first place, the political process is itself more complicated and problematical. Movements for social change may well begin in the literary and journalistic critiques of social ills. They may, as a next step, be able to secure a following among elites and the general public. Politicians may then perhaps take notice of their ideas and repeat their slogans. But it is a long way from that position to the adoption of public policy.

Coalitions must be formed with the other interests which compose American political parties. Some influence may thereby be exercised during the selection of a presidential candidate and on his election. After that, the group must secure presidential support for their policy. It must not be one of those presidents forget about or bargain away. In Congress, the group's friends must win influence in committees and caucuses. Personality conflicts and the usual give and take of legislative politics must be kept to a minimum. The opposition must be outflanked and one's supporters, most of whom will be lukewarm, kept from straying. Through House committee, House floor, Senate committee, Senate floor, conference committee, and House and Senate floors again the measure must run. During all of which, subcommittees, caucuses, congressional blocs, presidents, and other members of the administration have their possible actions factored into everyone's calculations. All the fluidity of personalities, electoral calculations, jockeying for position, and incessant compromises on varying issues introduce more uncertainty.

In short, it is more, I would contend, the political situation at any given congressional session that produces the policy outcomes than a deterministic reform/standpatter evolutionary conflict. Had the Republican party not split in 1912, it is unlikely the Democrats would have had the opportunity to have enacted an income tax immediately after ratification of the Sixteenth Amendment. Kitchin, being such a vociferous foe of preparedness in 1916 and war in 1917, cooled his relations with the administration. Wilson no doubt chose to let him have a free hand in tax matters to avoid the chance of his using his position to undermine the war buildup. Kitchin's and Simmons's insistence that the Republicans sit with them on a full committee to make substantive decisions altered the nature of consensus during the war. The approaching elections in 1916 and 1918 were of more than casual moment. Harding's leaving of tax matters to Mellon—indeed his choice of Mellon—affected the politics of 1921. The split within Republican ranks and Penrose's illness were also of importance that year. What this sample of idiosyncracies demonstrates is that the political prism is an uncertain conduit for the light of political reform.

In tax policy, more than most areas of public policy, it is the politics of a congressional session that is crucial,[3] for Congress has chosen to retain more control over tax policy than almost any other. The premier and singular role granted the House explains this in part. But it is also the fact that interest group politics is the norm except on rare occasions. Moreover, quite a few members of Congress have, or at least feel they have, a grasp of tax matters. Most of them after all are lawyers, businessmen, and farmers; they pay taxes and know others who do. Each revenue bill therefore will attract immediate attention and unleash all manner of political effusions. The battles will be intense because once a provision is in the revenue code, its opponents will have difficulty taking it out. Anytime, therefore, there is talk of general revenue revision, Congressmen and interest groups begin pushing their pet policy to the utmost.

It is not always clear, either, who wins. Mellon got reduced rates in 1921 but nowhere near the reductions he wished. In fact, in many ways he was soundly defeated, and at least one authority believes he was equally unsuccessful throughout the 1920s.[4] Was this really a retreat to "normalcy" and the opening salvo in a "decade of reaction"? The evidence seems to indicate otherwise. Did Kitchin and Simmons "win" by driving up surtax rates? It could be argued that they accomplished little if anything. In the complex that is Congress, drawing too rigid lines for inquiry may merely fog over the truth.

Moreover, the Progressive model sees the two sides as overly unified. It is basically true that "business" is an interest. But different segments of the business community also have different interests. Businesses come in all different sizes and types: some are suppliers of what others need; some prosper when others are hurting. Thus, on several tax issues business is hardly a united interest. Plus, it is not clear that business people know their own interest or that they pursue it, although admittedly this is less likely in tax matters.

More directly to the point in tax politics is the makeup of the other side. Progressivism was a multifaceted movement which had regional variations and crossed party lines.[5] In income tax politics southern gentlemen, rural midwesterners, northern urban workers, and western malcontents found common ground. They all favored progressive rates which fell more heavily on "eastern capitalists." But on other issues, even other tax issues, the coalition splintered. When the tax on child labor was offered as an amendment in 1918, southerners defected. (Their places were taken by more "responsible" East Coast conservatives and the amendment passed.) When it came time to discuss taxes on mining or the taxation of state and local bond interest, the westerners deserted in droves.[6]

If we accord the income tax a high place in the pantheon of bequests from the Progressive era, we must sadly note it is a legacy bequeathed only by racism. Were it not for the Democratic leadership in Congress being in the hands of those who wanted to spare the common man much of the taxes he bore in 1913, we would not have had the progressive income tax. But who were these economic humanists Ratner and others have praised? Kitchin, Simmons, Underwood, Hull, Williams, Garner. Every one of them was from the South, and they were all guardians of white supremacy. In fact, even their homilies on taxes are laced with crude racist stories and jokes. When they turned to such issues as black soldiers being armed during World War I or antilynch laws, their venom knew few bounds. To be sure, some were worse racists than others, and to be sure it can be argued that had they deviated from the "party line", their replacements might have been worse. And it is almost certainly true that without their votes and leadership we would have had much more exploitative tax policies. Yet, it is a sad tradeoff. Progressive tax policies were bought with impediments to any progress along racial lines. Before we celebrate the virtues of our income tax therefore, a tear is in order for those to whom taxes were secondary.[7]

In short, life and politics are complicated, and the good and the bad not always easily identifiable. A multitude of economic and political variables create a complex environment for tax policy makers. Treasury demands for revenue, conditions of inflation or depression, banking crises, wars, and so forth impinge on their thoughts. At the same time, elections and internal party politics generate another set of considerations. Moreover, unless we are totally cynical, we must believe principle has a place in all this. People in politics do believe certain things, or many of them do at any rate. When all these are mixed with the institutional structure of American government and the sheer economic and demographic diversity of the nation, we have tax policies that represent the best and the worst of the American character.

Models of the Tax Policy-Making Process

Discussing the applicability of various models of the policy-making process to different areas of substantive policy has long been a preoccupation of political scientists.[8] It is now generally accepted (although not by everyone) that there is not one "grand model" of policy-making. Instead, there are several, and the nature of the issue goes far to determine which prevails. A further refinement of this idea is the suggestion that different aspects of a single issue, or perhaps "subissues" is a better nomenclature, will also exhibit different models.

Rather, therefore, than one finding "a" model of federal tax politics, it could be that different portions of the revenue code are the outcome of different types of politics. If we look back over these first few years of the income tax's life, at least six different types of subissues can be seen, with several of them lending themselves to even further breakdown.[9]

Group one comprises issues which are a concomitant of income taxation itself. One set of these are obviously matters of rates. Are they to be progressive? If so, how much? Is the course of progression to be uniform? Is there to be an exemption? If so, how much? A second set of concerns here involves defining and classifying income. Examples are whether a distinction is to be drawn between earned and unearned income, whether capital gains are income, and the nature of "outside" transactions and their treatment. A third category consists of issues growing out of economic complexity and the diversity of business activity. Any method for defining income will inevitably produce disparities and incongruities for some lines of business, the prime example being the extractive industries. No matter what else the tax law does, therefore, it must address these issues.

A second group of issues is what I would call "small holes pointing to big holes." With some logic and usually with good intentions, a small hole is created for some set of taxpayers. Easily drawn examples from these years are the loss carryforward and carryback, the exemption for children, and the exclusion of clergy homes. The carryforward and carryback provisions have been extended and refined several times, always in the direction of more liberality. Under the "what is good for the goose" theory, this break for businesses was extended to individuals through the income averaging mechanism. The exemptions for children have grown in size and scope. It now encompasses dependents of all types, including those college-age children studying at parents' expense. A taxpayer even gets an extra exemption for himself and his spouse if either is over sixty-five or blind. The rule about clergy homes has likewise grown into a whole set of special rules for ministers and employees of religious organizations. For example, now ordained ministers who work for a church-related college (in any capacity) get to exclude the portion of their salary allocated to housing allowance.

Third, there are questions of fundamental public policy which are embedded in the tax law. Two examples in these years were allowing a deduction for charitable contributions and the development of tax expenditures such as the exclusion of veteran's benefits. It is at least debatable whether either of these groups deserves a public subsidy and certainly arguable even if they do whether utilization of the tax code is the proper way to go about it.

Fourth on the list is the linkage of the personal income tax with the corporate income tax. There must be a progressive income tax on corporations if partnerships and sole proprietorships are not to suffer discrimination. Yet, how to go about accomplishing the objective is one of the knottiest problems of economic and legal analysis. The 1980s find the situation no better than in the early days. There is now an "accumulated earnings tax," whose function it is supposed to be to force corporations to distribute their earnings. However, a corporation has an incompetent tax advisor if it cannot escape this trap. Justifications such as "future expansion" are difficult to challenge. Moreover, there are even special liquidations available to circumvent the bite if it appears to be closing in.

Fifth, there are issues of outright loophole closing. A glaring and well-publicized loophole, such as the altered basis for gifts and wash sales, is what I have in mind here.

Lastly, there are a few issues which if not addressed at the beginning will become more difficult to handle through time. The taxability of salaries of the president, federal judges, and state officials are examples, but the primary one of course is the exclusion of municipal bond interest from the income base. The salaries question was faced piecemeal, presidents and judges being brought in first and state officials somewhat later. But the bond interest question, after 1918, has remained off center stage. The policy has created two powerful interest groups. One is wealthy taxpayers whose marginal rates make these securities attractive investments. The other is state and local governments, who are able to sell bonds at much lower interest rates than would otherwise be possible. It has probably provided, therefore, for a larger set of capital improvements and much of our infrastructure of roads, bridges, schools, sewer and water systems, and other public facilities.

Removing the exclusion at this point would have uncertain consequences. Businesses needing capital would seem to benefit from an infusion of funds now tied up in municipal securities. State and local taxes would either rise or capital expenditures be curtailed. Since state and local levies are often regressive, it is not clear that the increased progressivity of the income tax gained by the move would offset the increased regressivity. The actual intake to the federal Treasury would be relatively small, so the magnitude of savings to others would be minimal. Perhaps, though, the easy availability of capital funds has led to irresponsibility at the state and local level. Necessary maintenance and replacement may have been forfeited because of the attractiveness of bond sales. Nevertheless, there is something fundamentally unjust about people with large fortunes escaping taxation. At the very minimum, the interest should be spread through the brackets. This would leave the constitutional issue untouched but allow the tax collector to come calling.

A look at the early handling of these issues, accompanied by the political science literature and substantial intuition (some would say these are the same), can give preliminary clues as to the style of politics in each of them. On the question of rates, for instance, there is always much debate and the repetition of platitudes.[10] Public interest and understanding is highest here. The matter appears simple, and much mileage is gotten from endless speeches. Those who favor lower rates at the top have repeated several versions of Mellon's argument but normally manage to convince only those already convinced. Those wanting steeper progressions have their own set of shibboleths. The infinite possibilities for compromise make the politicians' job somewhat easier. Both sides can make their appeals, forge a compromise, pretending to be holding their noses, and then blame the other side for the rates being too high/low whatever the economy does.

Issues such as earned versus unearned income and the capital gains tax are more complex. Consequently, public understanding is lower. These matters spark a lot of talk, though, and plenty of economic analysis. Seldom does the economic analysis policy makers repeat for public consumption amount to more than the enunciation of general principles. This does not detract, however, from press releases and press conference statements' solemnity, making them sound as though they are grounded in some complex argument. Both sides, it would appear, believe that justice and economic theory are on their side. Hence, there is a tendency for the policy to vacillate. We have drawn the earned/unearned dichotomy, repealed it, then replaced it. We have shortened the holding period for capital gains, lengthened it, and shortened it again. We have raised the capital gains rate, then lowered it. Ad infinitum. With the next election, it will change again.

In the third subset here, the provisions for diversity, there is an altogether different pattern. Once some favorable treatment has been granted, a special group is created which has a strong interest in seeing it maintained. The opposition is loose and amorphous. It cannot secure backing because no one is touched strongly enough. So what if the oil depletion allowance adds a few cents to everyone's gas and oil prices. Only when something pinches (e.g., lines at the gas pumps) and the provision can be attacked as a symbol do opponents stand a chance. Most of the time the accidents of politics smile more favorably on the special group. In oil's case Sam Rayburn's tenure as Speaker of the House was especially fortuitous. Supposedly, he asked every supplicant for membership on Ways and Means one all important question: Do you favor the oil depletion allowance?[11]

Turning to the small hole to big hole issues, there are two types of political process which yield this result. In one, seen in such cases as the loss carryforward and carryback and the exemptions, there is no special lobby to plead the cause. It appears to politicians the wise and equitable thing to do, whether because of general business or social conditions. The revenue impact of most of these moves is small at the time. That is, considering any current structure of either the loss carryforwards and carrybacks or the exemptions, mild extension will not devastate the Treasury. Over the years, the cumulative impact, however, is anything but minimal. But the popularity, especially of increased exemptions, is reason enough for elected tax policy makers to see wisdom in their adoption. As for matters such as excluding clergy homes, there are interest groups active. Allowing one part of a group to pay less brings a demand for the same privilege. In this case, ministers who received a cash allowance for housing were not absent from Washington for long. And the logic is irrefutable. Tax writers are not immune to appeals to such logic, and it is easier to grant the new claimant the exclusion than it is to reimpose the tax on the original taxpayers. So, in all these cases it is a politics of saying yes—because "yes" is easier than "no," there is seldom any opposition, and the revenue picture is only marginally affected.

On the third issue, we find a still different process. No one really wants to discuss the fact that a public policy question is being decided. Or if they do, they scrupulously avoid saying anything akin to "subsidy." Typically,the visible portion of the provision relates to some group with impeccable political credentials. Charitable organizations and veterans cannot be surpassed in that capacity. But they may not be the only beneficiaries. With the progressivity of the rates, the deductions or exclusions will be of vastly different value to different taxpayers. Hence the politics of this type issue means avoiding anyone's wrath. Enlarge the lists. Raise the maximum. Or, as was recently done, make charitable contributions even easier to deduct. There will be few opponents, and no open ones, to any of these moves.

In the politics of the fourth issue, three basic elements must be kept in mind. First, most people in upper income brackets are always seeking a tax shelter. Second, corporations vary tremendously in size and degree of diffusion of ownership. The real problem here is not with giant, publicly held corporations. It lies with the successful businessman whose wealth is miniscule compared to the Rockefellers' but dwarfs that of the average college professor. His medium-sized business is a corporation. (The reasons are several. The main tax one is that the highest marginal corporate rates have traditionally been lower than the comparable individual rates.) His family contains all the officers, and he (and probably they) draw handsome salaries. In most cases, he also has other investments on the side. What he can do is manipulate dividend payments to "get them out" when his income is lower. Third, as noted above, the problems are intractable.

As a result, the politics here are quite fluid. There is, I think, a genuine desire not to let it become a complete sham. Congress appears somewhat sensitive to the open and blatant manipulation of the revenue code. However, the Internal Revenue Service has been unable to enforce every attempt to frame a satisfactory solution; and the truth is no one has any idea how to handle it.

In fact, the anomalies of the corporate/individual linkage may produce a little hole to big hole situation. Corporations even smaller than the hypothetical one alluded to above, especially the closely held ones, have suffered the opposite penalty vis-à-vis partnerships and sole proprietorships. They have had to pay the corporate tax and then have their dividends taxed as ordinary income to the lone stockholder (subject to the modest dividend exclusion).[12] Plus, in the 1960s many states began allowing professionals to incorporate their practices. Congress, therefore, created the so-called Subchapter S to allow small corporations to be taxed in a manner very similar to partnerships. Like a balloon, though, Subchapter S has grown exponentially. It has become easier and easier to become Subchapter S. Moreover, as the individual and corporate rates have grown closer (especially in 1981), the attractiveness of Subchapter S has increased for medium-sized corporations. This has made for pressure to loosen the requirements still further, which Congress obligingly did in 1982.

On matters of all but outright evasion, group five, the sensitivities are again evident. In most cases, it is not the very wealthiest elite who are taking advantage of such a loophole. They usually have plenty of other ways of deflecting the tax man. Instead, it is the next tier of entrepreneurs and self-made half millionaires. So the political style is outrage and pious indignation. No one objects for fear of being in the position of defending loopholes. Most members of Congress probably sincerely believe they deserve more public appreciation than they get when they shut off these obvious shenanigans.

Concerning the last group, not much more needs to be said. The interest groups were created by congressional action, or more appropriately, inaction. They are not linked in any formal fashion, and they exercise influence at different access points. The wealthy elite prefer not to make a public issue of their tax break, fearing it would lead to populist-style attacks. But whether seen or not, it would be naive to believe they do not say something to somebody. State and local governments, on the other hand, have plenty of spokesmen in Washington, both inside and outside government. As important, a direction, a tone has been set. The longer the policy persists, the more it becomes institutionalized. Difficulty in mounting an attack rises as time proceeds. Unless there is a political uproar, it is hard to see where the pressure for taxation would come from. To be sure, there have always been and are a few who argue for full taxation, including all those who want comprehensive income taxation.[13] But after the first few years they have been unable to secure a serious hearing. Since it was not addressed in more fluid times, it seems likely we will have it for some time.

As the rates of income taxes have risen, many of these issues have become of even greater salience. Furthermore, as the income tax has eclipsed other federal levies in importance, its politics have assumed center stage. Its very complexity and the difficulty with which all income taxes are administered make for complex political processes. In the days of the tariff it was Byzantine, but everyone had the same goals and everyone's game was the same. When excises have been levied, all the players' goals and tactics were again similar. The income tax, in contrast, has all sorts of substructures and nuances. Its different provisions produce several different political configurations. When a general tax bill is being considered, they all operate simultaneously. There is some pluralism here, some interest group bargaining there, some special versus general interest over here, some politics of principle over there, some sacred cow pleading its cause to attentive ears in that corner, some politics of indignation in that one, some strange bedfellows over there, someone tuning his political antenna over here, and so on. There is, in sum, no one "politics of taxation," but several "politics of taxation."

The congressional sessions of 1913–21 were some of the most important ever for American public finance. They witnessed a debate over the major value questions of political economy, a designing of revenue bills with staggering totals compared to any previous experience, a grappling with thorny administrative and technical complexities, and the planning of a transition from a war economy to a peace economy. Through all these dimly lit paths, the makers of tax policy proceeded, giving, in the final analysis, an amazing stability and permanence to the income tax.

What is ironic is that most of these men viewed the income tax, for better or worse, as a tool to alter the economic structure of American society. In this effort, the effects have probably only been marginal: few economists would contend that it has either redistributed much income or inhibited much economic growth. On the other hand, the long-term political transformation it has wrought has been profound. Besides providing the wherewithal to fight a subsequent world war and underpinning the enormous expenditures made to finance the Cold War and the space program, it has altered the balance between Washington and the state capitals. Political interests have consequently flocked to the banks of the Potomac seeking to use the massive financial power of the federal government to support their projects. It is no accident that the first federal grant-in-aid program using the dollar matching formula (the Smith-Lever Act) was passed in 1914, or that the growth of this device has paralleled the growth of the income tax. Without the federal income tax, there is little doubt that our society would look very different.

It is perhaps no understatement, then, to say that these years were some of the most crucial in the nation's history.

NOTES

1. Sidney Ratner, *American Taxation* (New York: Norton, 1942).
2. A good summary of progressive historiography is Richard Hofstadter, *The Progressive Historians* (New York: Knopf, 1968).
3. A good review of the literature on tax policy making is Ronald King, "Tax Expenditures and Systematic Public Policy," paper presented at the American Political Science Association, 1982.
4. Benjamin Rader, "Federal Taxation in the 1920's: A Reexamination," *The Historian*, 33 (May, 1971), 415–35.
5. One of the best studies is John Buenker, *Urban Liberalism and Progressive Reform* (New York: Norton, 1973). For an overview see John Buenker, John Burnham, and Robert Crunden, *Progressivism* (Cambridge, Mass.: Schenkman, 1977).
6. It was in the capital-starved West that the greatest benefits were derived from low state and local bond interest.
7. The Wilson administration as a whole had anything but a progressive record in race relations. See Nancy Weiss, "The Negro and the New Freedom: Fighting Wilsonian Segregation," *Political Science Quarterly*, 84 (March, 1969), 61–79.
8. The literature is immense. A good overview may be found in Fred Frohock, *Public Policy: Scope and Logic* (Englewood Cliffs, N.J.: Prentice-Hall, 1979).
9. The defining attribute of these categories is political style. They are not really categories in the strict scientific sense for they are not mutually exclusive, nor I suspect exhaustive. Their only function is to be suggestive.
10. An excellent rendition of platitudes is Louis Eisenstein, *The Ideologies of Taxation* (New York: Ronald Press, 1961).
11. Quoted in Joseph Ruskay and Richard Osserman, *Halfway to Tax Reform* (Bloomington: Indiana University Press, 1970), 213.
12. Suppose a corporation has one stockholder and a fairly small net income. The owner draws a salary, which is deducted by the corporation but taxed as ordinary income to him. If he withdraws any more, it is dividends, not deductible by the corporation but also taxable to the recipient as ordinary income. So, compared to his competitor who is a sole proprieter, the net income paid as dividends is "taxed twice." Now, on the other hand, compare a four person partnership with a relatively high net income to a similarly fortunate corporation owned by four stockholders. The entire net income of the partnership is taxable to the partners whether distributed or

not. There can be no retaining of earnings, making further capitalization difficult. The corporation may, however, pay the four a salary (if they perform legitimate services), which is deductible. It may then retain earnings either for expansion or distribution at more propitious times for the owners.

13. This is the term employed by those who favor including all income in the base. See Joseph A. Pechman, ed., *Comprehensive Income Taxation* (Washington: Brookings, 1977). A critique of the idea can be found in William Fellner, *Problems to Keep in Mind When It Comes to Tax Reform* (Washington: American Enterprise Institute, 1977).

Epilogue
Some Personal Reflections on the Past and the Present

Although tax politics go on all the time, their place on the national agenda varies. In our own day, tax issues have once again surged to the front of attention. Ronald Reagan harped more than usual on tax themes in the campaign of 1980 and chose early on to make both the revenue and expenditure sides of the budget a central issue in his administration.[1] He proposed, and got, in 1981 a major tax reform act, the Economic Recovery Act of 1981. Although he had to swallow a few unwanted pills, the outlines of the law were his. A roaring deficit sent his administration into a tailspin and resulted in the Tax Equity and Fiscal Responsibility Act of 1982. Less his than the 1981 law, it still reverberated with policy lines drawn from his supporters.

What stands out most pronouncedly when contemporary tax politics are compared to 1913–21 is the degree to which the tax law is employed for ends other than revenue raising. While tax policy is always entangled in several webs, the assumptions of policy makers do serve to shape the priorities they attach to various goals. If there is a consensus on goals, there is still plenty of room for disagreement. Looking at the early years, it is interesting that there was a consensus that the first goal of taxation was providing governmental revenue. Both Democrats and Republicans in the executive and legislative branches adhered to this end throughout their struggles. What was sharply disputed was the distribution of the burden; what was not was that a certain sum needed to be extracted.

In the 1930s the notion of the federal budget being part of fiscal policy, I would argue, undermined the primacy of revenue raising. By the passage of the Full Employment Act of 1946, fiscal policy had become all but wedded to the accomplishment of macroeconomic objectives. As taxation became primarily a buttress to objectives of economic management, its politics underwent a further change.[2]

The political heirs of the Progressives, the postwar liberals, turned their interest toward the expenditure side of the budget. Social justice could best be secured through planting and nurturing institutions of the social service state. Especially in the 1960s, using federal expenditures to develop "human capital" was the thrust of reform. Tax policy became central only insofar as it was used to encourage economic growth. This was because it was only economic growth which could supply the needed social dividend.[3]

As many of these programs expanded beyond even the most generous projections, pressure on expenditure totals mounted. When coupled with escalating and then continuing costs of the Vietnam war, budget deficits grew. Few seemed interested in raising taxes to what would have been required to meet outgo. For a while the illusion lived on that deficits stimulated growth, that the important element was the ratio of the deficit to GNP, and that all would soon be well.[4]

More importantly, it deflected attention away from the justice of the tax burden itself. Of course, there were occasional laments by individual Congressmen or sometimes even the president about the unfairness of it all. But one is struck in reading the debates and writings of 1913–21 how clear this issue was to everyone, and how well accepted it was that it was the central issue. Who should pay? and How much?

Republicans then and now put forth the proposition that the wealthy should not pay much. It is the Democrats who have changed. By focusing on expenditure policy they have literally had their cake and eaten it too. They have been able to portray themselves as "compassionate" because they have pushed for expenditures to cover social programs for the disadvantaged. However, at the same time, they have been prone, in many of their own upper middle class interests, to make sizeable holes in the tax law. In January of 1983 an article in *The Washington Monthly* discussing the current shape of the party drove the point home.

What's worrisome about Manatt is not that he is wealthy and knows a lot of wealthy people. Until that far-off day when an Archibald Cox has been elected president and money has less power in politics, the Democrats will need good fund-raising. The question is, fund-raising and party-building by what breed of Democrat? What kind of Democrat does Chuck Manatt typify, and who does he attract to party activism? The issue is larger than Manatt himself.

One answer to that question lies in Manatt's creation of the Lexington Group, the Potomac Group, and the Hudson Group, all dedicated to bringing "young professionals" into active participation in the party. Isn't it possible that this segment is a tad overrepresented already? These are the people who cheered lustily as Edward Kennedy moved through the litany of liberal positions during his speech at the mid-term convention last June, but sat in silence—you could hear the hum of the air conditioner in the convention hall—when Kennedy criticized tax breaks that do nothing but create new work for lawyers. The reason for the silence was that Chuck Manatt and thousands of other Democrats *are* the lawyers, MBAs, accountants, consultants, and other professionals who profit from the system the way it is. Only a few weeks before, Manatt and the DNC's Business Council had sent a letter to Democratic congressmen essentially endorsing the most egregious of Reagan's 1981 tax giveaways, the so-called "safe harbor leasing" provision, which allows profitable corporations to buy the tax losses of unprofitable ones, thus lessening their tax bills.[5]

It is instructive to compare these modern day liberals with those early income tax advocates. In 1913–21, the coalition was made up of populist southerners, midwestern progressives, and westerners. Today the bastions of liberalism are the urban East and the posh sections of California. To a degree, this is a result of the fact that the East anyway has been most affected by the entry of immigrants and minorities into the political process. To an equal degree, though, it reflects the dominance of upper middle-class reformers. While they have a genuine sympathy for the less fortunate in our society, they have wedded that concern to all sorts of social issues which affect mostly themselves.

The consequences for tax policy are noteworthy. The very poorest have not fared too badly. Republicans have consciences too, and they have as often as Democrats generated tax concessions for those on the very bottom. (Remember the expanded exemptions in 1921.) The current earned income credit, for example, is supported by both parties. At the same time, the upper middle class and the upper class have created all sorts of safe havens for themselves. Democrats as well as Republicans cash in here too. What has happened is that the lower middle class wage earner and the middle middle class white collar worker and small businessman have been lost in the shuffle. They make too much to qualify for EIC, too little to make it worth having a tax accountant or lawyer manipulate their income even if it is not all wages and salaries, and they probably would not qualify for the most generous provisions anyway.

Most people who have examined tax policy and found it unjust have concluded only an informed and aware public can change it. I quote but one example.

> Perhaps what is needed more than anything else before a campaign for drastic tax reform can be launched successfully is a public that is better informed as to the inequities inherent in the present tax structure, so that it will become sufficiently aroused to exert relentless pressure for tax reform on its representatives in Washington.[6]

In a world of democracies functioning as high school texts say they should, this would be more encouraging. But the man and the woman on the street can play this role only indirectly. They cannot realistically be expected to give up football and gardening to study the intricacies of Accelerated Cost Recovery Systems, Subchapter S corporations, or safe harbor leasing. Political elites are necessary; it is rather a question of the values of the elite and how they carry those values out.

One segment of the political elite of 1913–21 related the plight of America's lower and lower middle classes directly to tax policy. They forced this issue, the distribution of the burden, to the center of attention and kept it there. Whatever their other defects, in tax policy they wanted the burden to fall a certain way, and they were vigilant to that end. In our day, there is only a faint echo of the values they elucidated.

As important as expenditures are, when they become the primary concern, justice cannot be done. Alternatively, of course, taxes cannot be divorced from expenditures. Both need to be assessed with that only certain guide to political action—a well thought out theory of justice. Until we discuss that openly at tax time, tax "reform" will be an illusion.

NOTES

1. See William Greider, *The Education of David Stockman* (New York: Dutton, 1982).

2. The best history of fiscal policy is Herbert Stein, *The Fiscal Revolution in America* (Chicago: University of Chicago Press, 1969).

3. The theoretical edifice rests on the existence of a Welfare Function in the economy. However, the growth of this W function ultimately depends on growth as traditionally defined. Discussions of welfare economics can be found in E. J. Mishan, *Welfare Economics* (New York: Random House, 1964) and Yew-Kwang Ng, *Welfare Economics* (New York: Wiley, 1980). On its applicability to expenditures, see Robert Millward, *Public Expenditure Economics: An Introductory Application of Welfare Economics* (London: McGraw-Hill, 1971).

4. See, for example, Walter Heller, *New Dimensions of Political Economy* (Cambridge, Mass.: Harvard University Press, 1966).

5. Jonathan Alter, "With Friends Like These . . . ," *Washington Monthly*, January, 1983, 18. Emphasis in original.

6. Joseph Ruskay and Richard Osserman, *Halfway to Tax Reform* (Bloomington: Indiana University Press, 1970), 218.

Index